HILLBILLY WOMEN

Hillbilly Women

KATHY KAHN

Photographs by Al Clayton
Migrant Photographs by Frank Blechman, Jr.

DOUBLEDAY & COMPANY, INC.
GARDEN CITY, NEW YORK
1973

ISBN: 0-385-01411-2
LIBRARY OF CONGRESS CATALOG CARD NUMBER 72–96246
COPYRIGHT © 1972, 1973 BY KATHY KAHN
ALL RIGHTS RESERVED
PRINTED IN THE UNITED STATES OF AMERICA

Grateful acknowledgment is made to Florence Reece for permission to reprint lyrics from her songs "Which Side Are You On?" and "We're Tearing Up an Old Recipe" Copyright © 1952 by Florence Reece. And to Sarah Ogan Gunning for use of her traditional song "Girl of Constant Sorrow."

The epigraphs beginning each chapter are lines from songs written by Si Kahn and Kathy Kahn, Copyright © 1973 by Si Kahn and Kathy Kahn.

Photo Credits: Photos 10, 11, 12 by Frank Blechman, Jr.; all other photos by Al Clayton.

For Si and our hillbilly babies, Simon and Jesse.

CONTENTS

CONTENTS

HILLBILLY WOMEN

MAP OF
SOUTHERN
APPALACHIA

Dellslow

Cincinnati

O H I O

W E S T
V I R G I N I A

OHIO RIVER

Fayetteville

K E N T U C K Y

Rodelle

Hazard

Goose Creek

Trammel

V I R G I N I A

Sneedville

Prathers Creek

Ellistown

T E N N E S S E E

N O R T H
C A R O L I N A

Copperhill

Hendersonville

McCaysville

Mineral Bluff

S O U T H
C A R O L I N A

Aska

Auraria

G E O R G I A

N

W   E

S

Atlanta

0   Miles   100

"I reached under my arm and I pulled out my pistol, and I walked out backwards. And I said, 'Martin, if you try to take this grub away from me, if they electrocute me for it, I'll shoot you six times in a minute. I've got to feed some children, they're hungry and they can't wait.'"

—AUNT MOLLY JACKSON

"God Almighty made the women and the Rockefeller gang of thieves made the ladies."

—MOTHER JONES

INTRODUCTION

This book tells what it means to be a woman when you are poor, when you are proud, and when you are a hillbilly. In it, nineteen hillbilly women tell their personal stories of the day-to-day struggle for survival in the Southern Appalachian Mountains. And in hillbilly migrant ghettoes in the North.

The women in this book come from all over the Southern mountains. Some of them were born and raised in the coal camps around Eastern Kentucky, Tennessee, Virginia, and West Virginia. Others have lived all their lives in cotton mill towns, factory towns, and farming communities in Tennessee, North Carolina, and North Georgia. All of them were raised in poverty in a rich and prosperous land. They are the daughters of coal miners, factory hands, and farmers, and they grew into hillbilly womanhood with a strong instinct for decency and dignity.

These women talk about life as a miner's wife, or daughter, or widow; of how it feels to be forced onto the welfare rolls because there are no jobs for women and your husband is disabled, and the bitter frustration of watching their land ravaged by coal and timber corporations. They tell of work in factories and cotton mills, of being ignored, manipulated, degraded, the subject of jokes and cartoons.

The women in this book have many things in common. They are the White Anglo-Saxon descendants of the pioneers who first settled the rugged Southern mountain land more than a hundred and fifty years ago. They have a pride in their heritage and their traditions. They have all spent most of their lives laboring under brutal living and working conditions. And, while they are proud, they are also angry with a country that makes their life a nightmare.

It was not until hillbilly music, or country music as it is called today, became nationally popular that many people began to take a second look at the hill people of the Southern mountains. And, if people are wondering where that music, with its undertones of sorrow and its sweet/harsh melody comes from, they can find the answer in the history of hillbilly people and their struggles.

Struggle has always been a major part of mountain people's lives. The women in this book represent, each in her own way, woman's resistance to the exploitation of her land and people. Some of the women are actively involved in movements to save the Southern mountains and its people from destruction and exploitation. They have organized unions, called strikes, walked picket lines, written protest songs, and marched on Washington. Others do not participate in organized resistance but show their dissatisfaction with their conditions in more subtle ways. But these accounts clearly indicate that hillbilly women are not content with the conditions of their lives.

Hillbilly women have a history of strength. Their land was first settled by English, Scottish, and Irish immigrants in the nineteenth century, who came to the Southern mountains to escape an oppressive British government. They were proud people and independent. They made their living from the land and passed down to their children a respect for family unity, for religion, and for music.

How mountain people came to be called "hillbillies" is not entirely clear. One theory traces the term back to British devotion to the name William. "Sweet William" is an English flower and many of the old British ballads had for their hero a young man named William. In the familiar ballad "Barbara Allen," for example, Barbara dies for Sweet William. In a later song the heroine's boy friend's name is "Common Bill."

Boys in the Southern mountains were often referred to as "Bill" or "Billy." And because they lived in the mountains they came to be called Hill-billies. Soon all those who lived in the Southern mountains began to be called hillbillies; it was a term used by the mountain people themselves and by outsiders. The term hillbilly is spoken with pride by mountain people to describe themselves, but it is a fighting epithet when used disrespectfully by outsiders to caricature and downgrade hillbilly people and their culture.

By the turn of this century, mountain people and their land were discovered by speculators from the North. Timber was discovered first, then bituminous coal, and finally Northern industrialists turned to the resource of cheap mountain labor. Coal companies sent agents into the mountains to buy the timber and mineral rights to the land from the farmers, paying as little as fifty cents an acre for the land. Then they moved in, dug deep mines, and hired mountain men off the farms to mine their coal and to cut their trees to make mine timbers.

Hoping for a more prosperous way of life, people left their

farms and moved to the coal camps. The coal companies paid low wages and provided the coal miners and their families with inadequate housing for which they collected high rents. It was not long before the dreams of prosperity turned into a nightmare of hard work and low wages under the rule of company bosses who regulated every aspect of coal camp life. And death in the mines became a daily occurrence. The coal camps around Tennessee, Eastern Kentucky, and the Virginias bred poverty and disease for coal mining families and riches for the coal operators.

The textile industry followed the coal companies to the Southern mountains to avoid dealing with unions in the North. Bypassing the coal region, where the male portion of the labor force was already occupied, textile companies established mills in the mountains of Tennessee, Virginia, North Carolina, and North Georgia. They built their company towns on the edge of the mountains and lured people off their mountain farms with promises of good cash wages.

The textile industry in the mountains employed whole families. Hillbilly men and women went to work carding, spinning, and weaving cotton in mills that were filled with dust and poorly ventilated. "Lintheads," as their bosses scornfully called them, worked ten and twelve hours a day to the sound of roaring machinery.

The wages in the mills were so low that families could not live off the income of one or two parents. Many families were forced to send their young children to work in the mills. The bosses welcomed the child laborers into the mills, thinking nothing of pulling them out of school and working them as hard as they worked their parents.

The mill villages and factory towns were identical to the

coal company towns. The company owned everything in town; the houses, the store, the schools and churches. Little cash money was seen by mountain people in company towns. Usually the company took a worker's paycheck, deducted for the house rent, for bills at the company store, and what was left went to the worker in the form of "scrip"—money privately printed by the company—which could only be used to purchase goods out of the company store.

The pride of making a living from the land was replaced with a servitude to coal and cotton. Hillbillies soon realized what the great coal and textile companies were doing to the land and people of Southern Appalachia. They began to fight back.

In the early 1900s the United Mine Workers of America began to organize coal miners in the Southern mountains. One of the union's strongest organizers was an elderly gray-haired lady. Her name was Mother Jones. She came to the Southern mountains from Ireland via Memphis, Tennessee, and Chicago. She organized thousands of coal miners to fight for higher wages and better working conditions. Mother Jones believed in the dignity of working people and she urged other women to join in the fight for working people's rights. She often told mountain women, "No strike was ever won without the support of the womenfolk."

Union organizing in the coal fields was bloody. During a strike of union miners at Paint Creek, West Virginia, in 1912, sixteen men were killed in a battle between the miners and company thugs. The following year the Imperial Coal Company hired gun thugs who rode a train through a tent city housing striking miners and their families. Two hundred rounds of ammunition were fired into tents occupied by men, women, and children. All over Eastern Kentucky, Tennessee, and West Virginia, miners were hunted down, beaten, and murdered because they fought to bring the union into the company towns.

The twenties were particularly violent years in the coal fields. Although the union was slowly gaining the upper hand over the coal operators, men were often out of work and they and their families were suffering from hunger and disease. Aunt Molly Jackson was a midwife in Eastern Kentucky during the twenties. She delivered babies and doctored families of union miners. One day, after seeing countless small children die of pellagra, Aunt Molly robbed a company store at gunpoint, taking enough food to feed a few families of starving children. She and her half sister, Sarah Ogan Gunning, wrote some of this country's finest labor songs. They were both eventually run out of Eastern Kentucky by the coal operators because of their organizing activities.

Florence Reece, who tells the story of early union organizing in the first chapter of this book, was another strong union woman and songwriter. She typifies the pride, the courage and the strength of the women in the coal camps. Her songs, written during the bloody times of the twenties and thirties, are sung today by organizers and working people around the world.

While the men and women in the coal fields were fighting the coal operators, textile workers in the South were beginning to organize their own unions. Their fight too was for higher wages, better working conditions, and the dignity of working people. And their battles were often violent.

In 1929 textile workers in Gastonia, North Carolina, struck the Loray Textile Mills. One of the union leaders, Ella Mae

Wiggins, the mother of nine children, was murdered as she and other strikers were riding along a public highway. A song she wrote called "Mill Mother's Lament" was sung at her funeral. In that same year, a group of women textile workers in Marion, North Carolina, were peacefully picketing their workplace demanding better working conditions. Six of the women were shot in the back and killed by National Guard troops.

Southern Appalachia was the scene of some of the most violent labor wars this country had ever seen until, through the efforts of Mother Jones and others, the UMW won bargaining rights for union miners. South of the coal fields, the Textile Workers Union hung on in several mill towns, but by the late thirties the great wave of organizing was over.

And then came the Great Depression when it seemed as if the country might not survive. Myra Watson recalls those days in her chapter of this book—when there were few jobs and "you didn't buy nothing out of the store," and corn liquor or "white lightning" became a profitable business in the mountains. The pure white whiskey is still available in the Southern mountains today, if you know the right folks, but most moonshiners are extremely cautious and a smart bootlegger never sells his whiskey to an outsider, because the outsider might be a revenuer.

During World War II and the decade following, industry fared well in Southern Appalachia. Workers were glad for any job, and employers enjoyed twenty years of relative calm while they built their empires and underpaid their labor. Men of wealth drove through their company towns in chauffeured limousines, while the men and women who labored in their mines and mills ate pinto beans and cornbread in poorly constructed company houses.

Even then there were not enough jobs in the mountains and some families headed for the cities of the North in search of jobs and a better life. Most of them found neither. Hillbillies made their home in the slums of Cincinnati, Chicago, Detroit, and Baltimore. They found their culture and mannerisms ridiculed by more affluent city people. They found themselves the subjects of cynical jokes and vicious caricatures. Others, in search of a new mountain land, migrated to the Pacific Northwest, to Washington and Oregon. There they found jobs in the coal mines and in the factories and in lumbering. But migration was never the answer to the problems mountain people face in their struggle for survival. Most hillbillies were reluctant to leave their Southern mountain home. And so they stayed on. For many of them it was a time of death: in the coal mines, in the mill towns, and on the battlefields of Europe, the Pacific, and, later, Korea.

Profits did not inspire the industrialists to improve working conditions and the workers continued to contract deadly occupational diseases in the coal mines and cotton mills. The McCarthy era, which spread fear and suspicion across the country, only served to make the struggle for working people's rights more difficult. And the memory of the bloody battles fought by their parents caused many hillbillies to wonder if the struggle was worth it after all.

The sixties saw the second wave of hillbilly resistance sweep through the mountains. John F. Kennedy was elected President of the United States and one of his promises was to return dignity to the people of Southern Appalachia. He became the idol of many hillbillies and his picture hung on the walls of shacks and cabins in even the most remote hollows of the mountains. Mountain people believed in Kennedy and were deeply angered by his assassination.

Lyndon Johnson's blueprint for the Great Society included plans for the people of Southern Appalachia. The Great Society literally made inroads into Appalachia. The federal government granted millions of dollars to the Appalachian Regional Commission to construct over a thousand miles of highways through the isolated mountains. Hundreds of families lost their homes to make way for highways built to attract new industry to the region. But the coal and textile corporations had a tight hold on the industrial market and they were not about to share their labor pool with other industries. The Great Society put Southern Appalachia on the road maps and left its people by the wayside.

Along with the Appalachian Regional Commission, the "poverty program" pointed to Southern Appalachia as one of the most concentrated areas of poverty in the country. Over a billion dollars of federal funds was pumped into the mountains in another political effort to convince America that the government intended to "eliminate the causes of poverty" and to give hillbillies a "head start" toward a new life. But much of the antipoverty money was handed down from one politician to another and much of what got past their pockets went into the pockets of the bureaucrats who ran the programs. Only a handful of poor people were helped by the poverty program and even then the help was superficial and temporary. The program failed because of many monumental errors, probably the biggest being that the federal government and the politicians who designed the "war on poverty" forgot to take human dignity into consideration. And, to hillbillies, a government that was hand in glove with the great corporations in Southern Appalachia was not likely to come to the aid of poor and working people.

Life for thousands of coal mining families had changed over the past twenty years, but not to the benefit of the workers. The mines were becoming more mechanized and thousands of miners were losing their jobs to machines that could mine as much coal as ten men. And the coal companies discovered a new way to take coal from the mountains, strip mining. The companies gave little thought to the land being ravaged by their giant bulldozers and the rivers they were polluting with wastes from the strip mines. It was just another way to make fast money and big profits as has always been the main concern of big corporations.

In the deep mines, as newer and faster machinery produced more and more dust, coal miners were increasingly developing and dying of black lung, or "miner's asthma," as it is sometimes called. The coal camps were filled with the widows and children of men who had died from black lung and mining accidents.

In 1964 the UMW was weak because of the loss of men through mechanization of the mines. There were few union mines left in Eastern Kentucky and wages for coal miners had dropped from twenty-four dollars to as low as four dollars a day. Once again, hillbillies took a hard look at what was happening to Southern Appalachia and its people. Throughout the coal fields in the sixties, people were saying, "It's time for a change."

One of the first protests of hillbilly people in the sixties was the "Roving Picket movement," an attempt by mountain people to strengthen the union in the coal camps. Granny Hager was a leader in that movement and she walked picket lines in the rain and snow trying to get coal miners to join in the strike for better working conditions and higher wages.

And although Granny was an important leader in the Roving Picket movement, she is rarely mentioned in accounts of it. The journalists who reported on the activities of the roving pickets failed to recognize the importance of the women involved in that movement.

For example, in the January–February 1968 issue of the magazine *Radical America* an article appeared on the Roving Picket movement which mentioned only the names of the male pickets and strike leaders and virtually ignored the participation of women like Granny Hager and others who were vital forces both within the rank and file and among the leadership.

In 1965 a tiny old lady named Widow Combs laid her body down in front of a bulldozer that had come to strip her land. She was sixty-one years old and she spent Thanksgiving of 1965 in jail. Widow Combs was one of the first mountain people to protest the destruction of mountain land by strip mining.

During this time several organizations were formed to protest conditions in the mountains. One of the largest groups, the Miners for Democracy, was organized by coal miners to fight the corruption within the leadership of the UMW. The Black Lung Association was organized by men who had black lung and widows whose husbands had died from it. In 1968 the seventy-eight widows of the Mannington mine disaster in West Virginia organized themselves and began a drive for mine safety. Their testimony before Congress helped secure the passage of the 1969 Mine Health and Safety Act.

Still the mines were rarely inspected and in December 1969, thirty-eight men were killed in an explosion at Hurricane Creek in Eastern Kentucky. Relief contributions had been received for the widows and families by a local civic group led by a county judge and his wife. Over thirty thousand dollars was donated from all over the country, but four months after the disaster, none of that money had been released to the widows. The widows were not allowed the time for quiet mourning; they were forced to fight for survival. They organized, demanded their money and got it.

While resistance was growing in the coal fields, the resistance to poor working conditions, low wages, and other injustices was mounting in the cotton mills and garment factories. In 1966 over four hundred female garment workers at the Levi-Strauss plant in Blue Ridge, Georgia, walked out on wildcat strike protesting the company's violation of seniority rights. Among those factory workers were Bernice Ratcliff and Lorine Miller, who tell about the Blue Ridge strike in their chapter of this book.

Today, in the seventies, there are close to six million poor and working-class people in the Southern Appalachian Mountains. More than half are women. Some hillbilly women are miners' wives; they live in the coal fields where there is almost no employment for women. The physical and emotional strength of coal camp women is a necessary force in the operation of the mining industry. Although a woman in the coal region of Southern Appalachia is not given much consideration by coal operators and county officials, her male kinfolk usually treat her with a good deal of respect because they can feel the contribution she makes both in the home and in the community.

If they had the opportunity, many of the women would probably go to work outside their homes, but as it is, women in the coal fields have accepted the role of wife and mother

14

and treat that role with respect. Although women in the coal fields are not financially compensated for their labors, they are very much a part of the work force in this country. Being a miner's wife means much more than the everyday drudgery of household chores and raising babies. It means struggling every day to eliminate coal dust from furniture, bed clothes, table tops, and children's bodies. It means being your own doctor because there isn't a clinic nearby and there is no money to pay for one anyway. It means giving children the only education they will ever get outside of a few inadequate lessons in poorly run schoolhouses. It means, most of all, waiting. The long hours when a coal miner is down under the earth in the mines are the worst hours for a miner's wife. Miners' wives know too well how easy it is to become a miner's widow.

In Tennessee, Virginia, North Carolina and North Georgia, women work in the factories and mills. Their jobs are for the most part routine and demeaning. The wages they take home are meager.

When a woman goes to work in a factory in the mountains, she is away from home for eight, ten, or twelve hours a day, five or six days a week. Once inside her place of work, she is at the mercy of the supervisors, the roaring machinery, and the rules and regulations of the company. In most factories, women are required to stay at their machines, sewing or spinning with no break, other than scheduled by the company, even to go to the bathroom or to stop for a cigarette and a cup of coffee.

The women are given a production rate, usually set by the pace of the fastest worker on the line, and are expected to produce at that rate or else they are fired. In sewing factories, many of the machines have clocks on them and the women are timed on their production. If a woman is sick, that is not considered an excuse for not meeting production quotas.

Many women physically shake when they are on the job because of the tension caused by having to meet production quotas. They often find it hard to control their hands as they operate their machines. Some women become so nervous at the end of a day's work that they can't eat, constantly drop things, talk incessantly, and lose their tempers easily. It is not unusual for these signs of nervousness to vanish during a week's vacation from their jobs. But the tension comes back with the job and usually increases and becomes more serious over the years.

For example, sleeve sewers working in a garment factory in North Georgia are expected to sew at least nine hundred sleeves during an eight-hour day. That averages sewing almost two sleeves per minute with no break for rest or lunch. If the women cannot meet this production for whatever reason, they are first reprimanded, then warned to speed up their work. Usually, if they fail after two weeks to meet production, they are fired. Nine hundred pieces of work in an eight-hour day is not at all an unusual required rate of production in Southern garment factories.

It is no surprise that so many women who work in factories have physical and psychological problems. Factory workers often take drugs, smoke incessantly when they are not at work, and many die at an early age. The cause is simple; factory workers are overworked and underpaid in one of the most nerve-shattering jobs in the country.

Workers in cotton mills work under much the same conditions as workers in sewing factories. There is one difference.

Like coal miners who slowly accumulate coal dust in their lungs, cotton mill workers are faced with the likely possibility that they will contract brown lung, a deadly disease, from breathing cotton dust. Some of the older mills are so dusty that card room workers can't see ten feet around them. Even in the newer, air-conditioned mills, there is a fine, invisible cotton dust that floats through the air and accumulates in the worker's eyes, ears, nose, throat, and lungs. And cotton dust, like coal dust, kills.

The women in this book remember death in the mines and death in the mill towns. They have watched their men die from black lung. Some of the women are suffering from brown lung from the cotton mills. They have fought in vain to convince the coal and textile corporations and the federal government that unsafe working conditions are a form of murder.

These are the women who are usually pictured in articles and books as mournful creatures, covered with dust and grime, their thin mouths hardened into a grim expression. Typically, the women are seen as hopeless, helpless, and passive. It is true that hillbilly women mourn, and like everybody who lives in a coal camp or mill town, they are covered with coal or cotton dust. And often their facial expressions are grim, like those of the women waiting to claim the bodies of their dead kinfolk at Buffalo Creek, Hurricane Creek, and Mannington.

Yet these women have put their lives on the line. They are the women who have blocked the giant bulldozers which still come to strip the land, destroy their mountains, and pollute their rivers. They have organized unions and led long and determined strikes. They have sheltered union organizers from company thugs. They have nursed starving children back to health. They are the hillbilly women who have marched to their statehouses and to Washington, D.C., who have told their elected representatives of the agonies of mountain people, only to have their words met by hollow promises.

It is no great joy for a woman to stay at home caring for children who any moment might be orphaned by a mine disaster. But neither is it gratifying to work the graveyard shift in a carpet mill like Burlington's Pine Tree plant in Dahlonega, Georgia. There is no great reward in spending ten or twelve hours a day weaving cotton gauze for Kimberly-Clark's tampons and Kotex, no excitement in sitting in the same spot all day long sewing identical denim pockets on identical denim Levi's. Nor is there much satisfaction in bringing home the entire family income when all that amounts to is three or four thousand dollars a year. Working women in Southern Appalachia know they are equal to their men in wages on most jobs, but they are not impressed. There is little status in being equal to $1.60 an hour.

The poor way of life is a tradition to hillbillies. To have been poor in the thirties is common; to have been poor and oppressed is something few people understand as well as mountain people. And to be poor, oppressed, and living in the technological seventies is an altogether new experience for the children of hillbilly coal miners, farmers, and factory workers. Technology with all its rewards to the wealthy has made it hell to be poor.

This book is about a culture and an identity which has been the subject of ridicule and scorn from Mammy Yokum and Daisy Mae to the Beverly Hillbillies. These are the White working women of Southern hill country, hillbilly kin to the "rednecks," "crackers," and "peckerwoods" of the Deep South and the "hicks" and "yokels" of the rural North. Like other minorities, they have had their fill of being ridiculed for the entertainment and profit of people who come from another place and another class. But hillbilly pride is not easily destroyed.

When hillbilly women talk about liberation, they are talking about the liberation of their people from the class system in this country which makes it possible for a few men and women to be comfortable while the rest of the people are forced to fight among themselves for what is left. Hillbilly women need to be liberated. They need to be freed from the bonds imposed on them by a society that is reaping the benefits of their land and labors. But, like most working-class women, they will never fall prey to the media-created fads which advertise themselves as "women's liberation." Hillbilly women are real feminists, they have a history of fighting for the rights of working women in the Southern mountains. But they are also humanists. They are fighting for the liberation of all people.

I chose the women for this book because they are all proud to be hillbilly women. I believe this pride is representative of mountain women. And too, I chose them because they are angry. Most hillbilly women are angry at their conditions, though many may not show it as obviously as these women do. There are no middle-class women in the book because most women in Southern Appalachia are either poor or working class. And there are no Black or Indian women. This is the story of their class-kin, poor White women.

Each of the chapters in this book is a life story, or part of one, told to me by the woman who lived it. I have tried to cover most of the major issues that affect hillbilly women's lives; like coal, cotton, working and living conditions, religion, music, family and kinship ties.

I have not chosen to give equal time to the antagonists. The corporations and politicians attacked in some of these accounts have very sophisticated ways of getting their story to the public. I could not have written *Hillbilly Women* from any other point of view than that of an activist in the struggle for working people's rights. But my point of view does not affect the truth of what is told here.

I met most of the women you will meet in this book through my personal involvement in organizing working people. It was because of my experience as a working-class woman that I developed the anger that prompted me to write this book. And it was the strength and courage of these women and others like them that gave me the motivation to complete it.

I was raised in a large family and although we never knew poverty, I recognized that my parents had to work very hard to support us. I was introduced to the ranks of working-class women when I was seventeen. Knowing my parents couldn't afford to buy me a college education, I went to work on various unskilled jobs, hoping I could make enough money to pay for an education. I worked as a salesgirl in department stores, as a waitress, in an electric parts factory. I worked in a beauty shop, sweeping up the shorn locks of wealthy women. I usually worked twelve to fourteen hours a day, six days a week. My wages averaged around $1.25 an hour, but often I was never paid for working overtime. It was just expected that I give my time to the company.

Being a working-class woman means being stepped on,

pushed around, degraded, overworked and underpaid. More than that, it means you have little hope that you will do anything more in life than a lot of hard work. If you have talent and ability it goes unrecognized. I gradually built up a deep anger inside me at the conditions of myself and other working people. At the same time I recognized there were other people much more maligned than myself. My anger at the system that allows only the wealthy and powerful to have human dignity led me to walk off my job and start getting involved in the struggle for change.

I have spent the last ten years organizing poor and working-people's groups. In simple language, that means working together with other people to try to change the balance of power and wealth, working for everybody's right to human dignity. The importance of community organizations, or poor people's organizations, working-people's unions is that people with common problems can work together sharing their ideas, their talents, and their skills in the struggle against their oppressors.

I have worked with many of the women in this book on such issues as black lung, mine health and safety, organizing factories and people's cooperatives, welfare rights, health conditions in the cotton mills. This book comes out of my experiences with these women and many other people in the South who are working for people's rights.

Although these women share many of the same feelings and hopes, they are isolated from each other by the rugged mountains and the first time most of them will meet will be in the pages of this book.

Myra Watson was the first person I interviewed for *Hillbilly Women*. It was a simple kind of interview. We just sat down on the front porch of her house one day and talked to each other, taping the conversation as we talked. Her words are just as she spoke them.

The process was much the same with the other women. Some conversations were easier than others. For instance, Ellen Rector and I had the luxury of talking in a room by ourselves. But when I interviewed Daisy Messer and Betty Messer Smith, it was in the middle of a knockdown, drag-out political battle, and while we were taping we were constantly interrupted by the opposition's attempt to turn off our electricity. Often there were children present. Their play made some of the tapes difficult to transcribe but added an important sense of reality to our conversations.

Some of the women were used to being interviewed. Florence Reece has been the subject of many newspaper and magazine articles. But most of the women were honestly surprised that I found their lives interesting enough to write about. When I first asked Katherine Tiller to be a part of the book, she suggested I interview her husband, John, instead. When I explained that the book was about women, she gave a very moving account of her life.

After I finished an interview, I took the tape home and transcribed it. Then I edited it to make a chapter for the book. I sent each chapter to the woman, and she read it over and made any changes she wanted to make. Altogether, it took about two years to complete the book. I have called it *Hillbilly Women* because hillbilly women are proud of what they are. I hope the lives of these women will provide other hillbilly women with a sense of their own unique history. I hope they will serve as a point of identity for all women who are seeking to learn about themselves. This book says that hillbilly women who are angry about their conditions are the rule rather than the exception. And perhaps by openly discussing subjects like illegitimacy, widowhood, courtship, sex, oppression, poverty, and war, it will be easier for hillbilly women to talk to each other about their problems and their lives.

If the struggles of these women do not stir people then this book has failed. Parts of the book will undoubtedly embarrass certain coal operators, politicians, and mill owners. But I do not expect them to be moved by accounts of hardship, suffering, disability, and death, since they have not reacted to these conditions when confronted by them face to face. I know that they won't understand the good times mountain people have, because they do not understand the joys of hillbilly life. There is a joy in family gatherings, in music and religion, and in helping each other. That joy and strength and perseverance shine through the lives of these nineteen strong and beautiful women who have lived for other people in the traditional hillbilly style.

I hope that those who read about these women will take to heart what they say and that the women themselves will never forget that they have shed a bright light on the beauty which is their own, and have made it possible for others to understand the strength, the courage, and the humility that makes each of these heroines proud to be a hillbilly woman.

Kathy Kahn
MINERAL BLUFF, GEORGIA

Part One

GIRL OF CONSTANT SORROW

I AM A GIRL OF CONSTANT SORROW
BY SARAH OGAN GUNNING

I am a girl of constant sorrow,
I've seen trouble all my days.
I bid farewell to old Kentucky,
The state where I was born and raised.

My mother, how I hated to leave her,
Mother dear who now is dead.
But I had to go and leave her
So my children could have bread.

Perhaps, dear friends, you are wondering
What the miners eat and wear.
This question I will try to answer,
For I'm sure that it is fair.

For breakfast we had bulldog gravy,
For supper we had beans and bread.
The miners don't have any dinner,
And a tick of straw they call a bed.

Well, we call this Hell on earth, friends,
I must tell you all good-bye.
Oh, I know you all are hungry,
Oh, my darling friends, don't cry.

They Say Them Child Brides Don't Last

FLORENCE REECE
ELLISTOWN, TENNESSEE

Wake up, wake up, you working folks, what makes you sleep so
    sound?
The company thugs are coming to burn your homeplace down.
They're slipping around that mountain town with guns and
    dynamite
To try to murder the sleeping folks that led the Harlan strike.

During the union organizing of the twenties and thirties in the Southern coal fields, several songs were written about the struggle by women who were going through it. Sarah Ogan Gunning was a miner's wife in Harlan, Kentucky, and she wrote the famous song, "I Am a Girl of Constant Sorrow." Aunt Molly Jackson, a midwife in Bell and Harlan counties, wrote many songs, including one called, "I Am a Union Woman." One of the verses to that song goes like this:

The bosses ride big fine horses,
While we walk in the mud.
Their banner is the dollar sign,
While ours is striped with blood.

The women used their songs to organize coal mining families into the union. They were one of the most effective
organizing tools because they captured the spiritual, emotional,
and physical feelings of people who were dying of starvation
while they fought some of the bloodiest battles union organizing has ever known.

Perhaps the most famous song coming out of that time is
"Which Side Are You On?" which Florence Reece wrote
while she and her husband, Sam, were organizing miners in
Eastern Kentucky.

The songs of Florence Reece, Aunt Molly Jackson, and
Sarah Ogan Gunning brought spirit to coal mining families
during their time of hardship and struggle. Today, they recall vividly just how brutal those times were for the people in
the coal fields of the Southern mountains.

Sam went in the mines when he was eleven year old.
Sixty cents a day. And there wasn't no such thing as hours.
He'd come out of there way in the dark of the night. And
him just a little boy.

As soon as a boy'd get up to be ten or eleven year old,
he'd have to go in the mines to help feed the others in his
family. As soon as he got sixteen year old, he'd marry and
it'd start revolving over.

I was fourteen when we got married and Sam was nineteen. Child bride. They say them child brides don't last, but
they do. When the gun thugs was coming around we had

eight children. We had ten altogether. And every one of them was born at home.

My father was killed in the coal mines. He was loading a ton and a half of coal for thirty cents, and pushing it. And that's what he got killed for, for nothing. That was Fork Ridge, Tennessee; they call it Mingo Holler now.

In the morning when they'd go to work before daylight, you could see the kerosene lamps they wore on their hats. It was just like fireflies all around the mountain. They'd go under that mountain every day, never knowing whether they'd come out alive. Most every day they'd bring out a dead man. Sometimes, two or three.

I never knew where Sam would come out of the mines alive or not. I've seen him come home and his clothes would be froze into ice. He'd have to lay down in the water and dig the coal, and then carry a sack of coal home to keep us warm and to cook. But he had to go, had to go somewhere cause the children had to eat. Sam joined the union in nineteen and seventeen.

Well, it was in Harlan County, Kentucky, and they was on strike. John Henry Blair, see, he was the High Sheriff, and he'd hire these men to go and get the miners. He'd hire these men that was real tough, and they'd give them good automobiles to drive and good guns to carry and they'd give them whiskey to drink, to beat the miners down, keep them down so they couldn't went in the union. They called these men "deputy sheriffs" but they was gun thugs. That was the coal operators with John Henry Blair.

We was living in Molus in Harlan County, Kentucky, then. In 1930 the coal miners went out on strike against the coal operators. Well, Sam had a garage down below where we lived. The miners would come there and hang out and talk about how they wasn't going back to work. So some of the bosses and officials come and asked Sam if he'd go back to work and Sam said did that mean that they got the union contract. And they said no. So Sam said, well, he wouldn't go back to work. From that beginning they started on him.

First, they arrested him, they took him to jail, said he was selling whiskey, anything they could put on him. And he wasn't fooling with whiskey at all, no, not at all. That was in nineteen and thirty.

It seems like a bad dream when you think about it, that it happened to your own children. They didn't have no clothes, nor enough to eat, they was always sick and you could see they was hungry. We was all just starving, and so the miners would go out and kill cows or goats or just anything. They belonged to the coal companies, you know.

I've seen little children, their little legs would be so tiny and their stomachs would be so big from eating green apples, anything they could get. And I've seen grown men staggering they was so hungry. One of the company bosses said he hoped the children'd have to gnaw the bark off the trees.

In Molus they didn't have nothing to eat. The miners and their families was starving and a lot of people had that pellagra. One woman come to my house to get something to eat and she had that. All scaly all over, you know. Someone said, "Aren't you afraid you'll catch that from her?" I said, "No. She got that at the table cause she didn't have no food."

While we lived in Molus and Sam was away, he wasn't

just hiding from the gun thugs. He was organizing with the union. One time he was gone a week and I didn't know where he was dead or alive. Well, one night he slipped in way long about one o'clock in the morning. We had a garden, it had corn and he slipped in through the back way, up through the corn. And I stayed up all that night watching for them to come after Sam.

The thugs made my mind up for me right off, which side I was on. They would come to our house in four and five carloads and they all had guns and belts around them filled with cartridges, and they had high powers. They'd come here looking for Sam cause he was organizing and on strike.

One night they killed eleven. That was "Evart's Fight." That was in May of 1931. It was at the Greenville crossing. A little boy heard the thugs a-talkin', saying they was going to meet the miners there at the railroad crossing and kill them. This little boy run and told his daddy and his daddy run and told the miners. The miners was there to meet the gun thugs and killed seven of them. Four miners got killed in the fight and the rest of them got sent to the penitentiary. One of them was a Negro man. But the thugs, they didn't get nothing.

Do you remember Harry Simms? He was from New York, he was a organizer. Sam was in the holler with Harry Simms, and Sam had just come out when the thugs backed Simms up on a flatcar and shot him. Well, the miners took him to Pineville after he was shot and he bled to death on the steps of the hospital. They wouldn't let him in cause he was a union man. They killed Harry Simms on Brush Creek. He was nineteen year old.

The gun thugs would take the union men out and kill

them. The miners would go out in the woods and the cemeteries and hide. So then they had the state militia out after them. We'd find men's bones up there on Pine Mountain where they'd take them out and shoot them.

There was one man, a organizer, he come to our house. His back was beat to a bloody gore, he was beat all to pieces. He took off his shirt, went out back and laid in the sun for a long time. He stayed here all day. We pleaded with him not to go back. But he says, "Somebody's got to do it. I'm going back." When one gets killed, somebody's got to go back and take his place a-organizin'. And he went back and we never heard from him again.

One old man come to our house. Dan Brooks. They had a thousand or two thousand dollars on his head. I kept him in our house. He come in here from Pennsylvania to organize. He stayed two nights then left for a day. Then he came sneaking back to the house and that night he held a meeting on our porch. He told the miners, "Somebody's got to lose their lives in this, but won't it be better for them that's left?" And that's right. If we lose our lives a-doin' something like this, struggling, trying to get higher wages and better conditions for the workers, better homes, schools, hospitals, well then, if they kill us but yet if the people get those things, then it'd be better that we'd lose our lives for what'd help the workers.

Well, the thugs kept coming and coming. One day Sam went down to the garage and I saw them coming. I knowed from what had happened to other people that they was going to search the house.

Sam had a shotgun and he had a high power. Well, I was setting on the porch with my baby. They come on in and

I got up and went in after them. My eleven-year-old daughter got that shotgun and that rifle and jumped out the window and ran, went up in the cornfields and hid.

We had shells hid inside the record player and I didn't want them to get them cause Sam would go hunting, you know. Well, one of them started to play the record player . . . it was one of them old ones you got to crank . . . he started a-crankin' it. I said, "You can't play that. It's broke." "Oh." And he stopped cranking it. I knowed if they'd started a-playin' it they'd've killed every one of us cause there was shells in there.

They looked in the beds, under the beds, through the dirty clothes, through folded clean clothes. Said they was a-lookin' for guns and literature. I'd never studied papers, I'd never heared tell of the International Workers of the World till they come, I didn't know what it meant. So that worried me. I told them, I said, "I'm not used to such stuff as this. All I do is just stay at home and take care of my children and go to church." One of them said, "As long as these communists is in here, you'll have trouble." I didn't even know what a communist was, I never heared tell of a communist before. But every time a body starts to do one good thing, he's branded a communist.

So they kept harder and harder a-pushin' us. One day when Sam was gone, they come with high powers and a machine gun. They come down the back road they was a-guardin'. They was intending to get Sam. So I sent my son and my sister's son down the front road to Bell County to tell the miners not to come, the gun thugs was a-waitin' on them. The thugs didn't get nothing that time.

But then they was back again. Says, "Here we are back."

I said, "There's nothing here but a bunch of hungry children." But they come in anyway. They hunted, they looked in suitcases, opened up the stove door, they raised up the mattresses. It was just like Hitler Germany.

Down at that little garage we had, there was a man that worked there, his name was Tuttle. The gun thugs thought he was so dumb he wouldn't listen at nothing, he was all dirty and greasy. Well, Tuttle heared something and come up and told me. Said, "They're going to get you or Harvey"—Harvey was my fourteen-year-old son—"and hold one of you till Sam comes." Well, I couldn't wait for nothing. Harvey was up at Wallens Creek tending to Sam's chickens and Tuttle went up there, told Harvey they was coming to get him. So Harvey come back down to the house. I told him, "Harvey, the thugs is going to get you or me and hold until your Daddy comes. Now," I says, "you go to Mrs. Brock's and tell her if she'll keep you all night till you can get out of here, I'll give her anything in my house, anything. And," I said, "tell her not to let them know you're there."

Well, he went. But he didn't stop at Mrs. Brock's at all. He went right on through the woods. The stooges was always a-watchin' the house and they saw him a-goin'. So Harvey walked eighteen miles through the woods, him fourteen year old. And they followed him along, these stooges did.

The next morning we was a-movin' out of our house, getting out fast. Tuttle was a-helpin' us and he was scared to death. So we come on down to Mrs. Brock's and we couldn't see Harvey nowhere. She said she hadn't seen him at all, he hadn't been there. We figured they got him between our place and Mrs. Brock's.

Well, we went down to Pineville. We called at the hospitals and the jails a-lookin' for Harvey. But we couldn't find him. So we went down to our friends, the Dilbecks. I said, "Has Harvey been here?" He says, "Yes, he come here last night and we put him in the bed. And," he said, "he'd got up and left it was peeping daylight." We went on then, with all our things, and made it to the Tennessee-Kentucky line. There, on the Tennessee side, a-settin' on the fence was Harvey a-waitin' on us.

I was thirty when I wrote "Which Side Are You On?" We couldn't get word out any way. So I just had to do something. It was the night Sam had sneaked in through the cornfields and I was up a-watchin' for the thugs to come after him. That's when I wrote the song. We didn't have any stationery cause we didn't get nothing, we was doing good to live. So I just took the calendar off the wall and wrote that song, "Which Side Are You On?":

WHICH SIDE ARE YOU ON?
BY FLORENCE REECE

Come all you poor workers,
Good news to you I'll tell,
How the good old union
Has come in here to dwell.

(Chorus:)
Which side are you on?
Which side are you on?

We're starting our good battle,
We know we're sure to win,
Because we've got the gun thugs
A-lookin' very thin.

(Chorus:)
Which side are you on?
Which side are you on?

If you go to Harlan County,
There is no neutral there,
You'll either be a union man
Or a thug for J. H. Blair.

(Chorus:)
Which side are you on?
Which side are you on?

They say they have to guard us
To educate their child,
Their children live in luxury,
Our children almost wild.

(Chorus:)
Which side are you on?
Which side are you on?

With pistols and with rifles
They take away our bread,
And if you miners hinted it
They'll sock you on the head.

(Chorus:)
Which side are you on?
Which side are you on?

Gentlemen, can you stand it?
Oh, tell me how you can?
Will you be a gun thug
Or will you be a man?

(Chorus:)
Which side are you on?
Which side are you on?

My daddy was a miner,
He's now in the air and sun,*
He'll be with you fellow workers
Till every battle's won.

(Chorus:)
Which side are you on?
Which side are you on?

The music to the song is an old hymn. I can't remember
what was that hymn, but I've got to look in the songbooks
and find out what that was a tune to.

Now, I got a song, I like it, a lot of people like it:

We're tearing up an old recipe
Of poverty and war
We don't know why we're hungry
Nor what we're fighting for.

This old recipe is yellow with age
It's been used far too long
People are shuffling to and fro
They know there's something wrong.

If the sun would stand still
Till the people are fed, all wars cease to be
Houses, hospitals, schools a-built . . .
We must have a new recipe.

Sam says it's better I don't have music with my songs
cause then they can understand every word you're saying.
When you're past going out and organizing, well, then
maybe you can sing a song or write a song to help.

Sometimes I can cry, and sometimes I get hurt too bad,
tears won't come. I cry inside. It hurts worse. The ones that
don't want the poor to win, that wants to keep us down in

* Blacklisted and without a job.

37

slavery, they'll hire these gun thugs, like they did over in Harlan County, to beat the workers down. And all in the world we people wanted was enough to feed and clothe and house our children. We didn't want what the coal operators had at all, just a decent living.

The workers offered all they had. They offered their hands, most of them offered their prayers, they'd pray . . . well, they'd also drink moonshine. But they was good, them coal miners.

How I Got
My Schoolgirl Figure Back

GRANNY HAGER
HAZARD, KENTUCKY

I had a dream the other night as plain as it could be
I dreamed the Heavenly City was run by working folks like me.
Oh what a joy that day would be, no greater anywhere
That union local number one, in heaven so bright and fair.

Granny Hager lives on the other side of the tracks. Whenever she goes out, she must cross the railroad tracks to reach
the road. And the only way she can get back home is to cross
back over again to the other side. For Granny, crossing the
tracks is no simple matter.

Some time ago the L&N Railroad, which hauls coal out of
Eastern Kentucky, began parking their coal cars in front of
Granny's house, moving them only once every few days and
then only temporarily. So, to reach her house Granny has to
slide between the cars at a joint or crawl under a car, her body

parallel to the tracks. Should the cars suddenly jerk forward she would be killed instantly. An interesting form of harassment against a radical old lady by a railroad company closely linked to the coal corporations of Eastern Kentucky. But obstacles are nothing new to Granny and neither is harassment.

Born and bred in the coal camps of Eastern Kentucky, Granny has always known the oppression of the coal operators who gouge their millionaire bankrolls from the mineral-rich mountain soil, who operate mines that are unsafe, deathtraps to hillbilly coal miners. These are the mines that kill and maim thousands of men each year. They are the mines that killed Granny's husband, Ab Hager.

Ab Hager died of pneumonicosis, or "black lung," the dreaded coal miners' disease caused by the black dust from the bituminous coal mined in Southern Appalachia. Gradually this dust fills a coal miner's lungs until there is no capacity for breathing and he dies of suffocation. Death comes after years of long, slow suffering. There is no cure, although the disease can be prevented by dust control—as it has been in every Western coal mining nation except the United States. This investment into the lives of coal miners would cost the coal barons money and decrease their corporations' profits. And so, despite the passage of the Mine Health and Safety Act of 1969, coal operators have done almost nothing to improve conditions in their mines.

In the early sixties, shortly after Ab's death, Granny and thousands of other Eastern Kentucky mountain people reached the end of their tolerance of the injustices leveled against them by the coal operators. In 1962 a spontaneous drive by mountain people resulted in the formation of the Appalachian

Committee for Full Employment. The purposes of the Committee were to end job discrimination in the coal mines, to strengthen unionization of the mines, and to improve the working conditions of coal miners in Eastern Kentucky.

Led by Granny and a retired coal miner named Ashford Thomas, "roving pickets" went from coal mine to coal mine calling for the miners to come out on strike until their conditions were improved. The roving picket movement was marked with threats and violence from the start and Granny soon became a veteran at dealing with harassment.

At one time we was solid union here. But what the coal operators did, they would come around and say, "Well, boys, I'm losing money, I just can't work it this way. If you all will take a cut, we'll work on, and if you don't, we're going to have to shut down."

Naturally the men would take a cut. First thing they knew, they were down to working for nothing. They were working for seven, eight dollars a day. And that's the way the coal operators busted the union and got the men to work for nothing.

So we set up. I believe it was about '62. We set up the Appalachian Committee for Full Employment. The United Mine Workers Union in New York sent a man in here, to see what we could do undercover, see if we could get the miners organized and then bring it all out in the open.

We talked up this roving picket idea, and we went to work. Where we knowed there was un-union mines, we went in time enough to catch the day shift as it went in and the night shift as it went out. We'd ask the miners to sign the checkoff, to come out with us for more money. Well, most of them would sign it, you see, and they'd turn around and go back home, they wouldn't go back in the mine.

One morning real early, we decided to leave out from the union hall in a motorcade and go out and picket. We left the union hall at two-thirty that morning to hit Southeast Coal Company in Knott County. Me and Ashford Thomas, we was riding in the front car and we dropped in over there. But when we'd got about fifteen miles from the mines, the snow was just about that deep and that high. And, boy, did we have a narrow road to drop down into the mines.

So me and Ashford and the rest went on. Whenever nobody else wouldn't ride in the front car going in, me and Ashford, that was all the sense we had, we'd take the lead. So we caught the night shift as it went out and the day shift as it went in.

Well, Southeast, they was a hundred and thirty-seven men a-workin' up there. We asked them to sign the check-off. And a hundred and thirty-six of them signed it and come back with us. There wasn't but one that wouldn't sign it.

So now the UMW was supposed to give the union men each a twenty-five-dollar check. And from then on the union was supposed to give them fifty dollars a week to feed their families on as long as they stayed out.

That evening we went back on down to the union hall. We'd always go down there after one of these runs and make our plans for the next morning. Well, we decided we'd hit Charley Combs's mine over on Big Creek the next morning.

When the morning come, we changed our mind and decided to go back up the other way again. So back we went, but we didn't do so good this time.

Just as soon as we got out of the driveway at the union hall, they was a whole bunch of highway patrols fell in behind us. And they cut in between our cars. They tried to arrest Ashford. He walked down to their car and they said something or other smart to him. He told them, he said, "If you were standing out there and helping us fight for our rights you'd be better off, instead of guarding scabs for them to go in the mines and work."

Well, one word brought on another, and one of them highway patrols, he jumped out. He said to Ashford, "I'll knock your brains out and put you in that car." Ashford, he said, "You'd better get somebody to help you." He was a little bitty gadget, but it took three of them highway patrols to put him in that car. And they started off to Whitesburg with him. They got about three miles from Whitesburg and the patrol stopped. They said, "Now, Mr. Thomas, we're going to let you go back home. But we don't want to catch you on nary another picket line." Ashford said, "If that picket line's down there when I get down there, you'll catch me in it. And if it hain't," he said, "you'll catch me in the first one that leaves in the morning."

And we had a snoop somewhere in the bunch from then on. We'd say we was going one place and then the next morning we'd head out for another place, trying to throw the highway patrols off. But, the next morning when we formed that motorcade, they knowed exactly where we was going and they would tell us so. We never did catch the one that it was.

43

We wasn't getting nowheres fast, you see, because we had somebody a-sneakin' on us. So at one meeting everyone had their say about it. I'm always the least sayer in the bunch; I'm the biggest mouth, but when I get up I hain't got much to say. Well, I got up. Berman Gibson said, "Granny, you look like the devil." I said, "I *feel* like the devil. I'll tell you the truth, it's got to be a man that's tipping the thin gray line off to us." That's what they call the highway patrols here. "If we find out who that man is, we don't want none of the men in our way." I said, "All you women that'll help me take him out of here, hold your hands up." They every one of them women held their hands up. And we really meant it; as much as we'd went and starved and suffered and waded in the snow and stood in it. I really meant I would try to take him out of there, and I knowed with a little help I could.

Well, Berman Gibson, he took over to handle the union's money, a-goin' to get it and paying these men. Well, the men never did get more than twenty-five dollars, but we knowed it was supposed to be more. So the men figured we wasn't going to make it, we wasn't going to accomplish nothing. Gradually the men started going back to work, on account of their families suffering, they couldn't stay out on twenty-five dollars. The International wouldn't come to us until all the men all over Perry County come out. If we could have got them out then the UMW might have come to us.

We never did get a union back in here. It's still here in some of the mines, but it's not carried out like it should be. In other words, it's a bunch of dues-paying scabs, is what we call them. These little mines still work for whatever they want to pay them.

One morning, the day after one of our meetings, I got up and somebody had set fire to some pine grass out there by the bathroom—I've always had to have a outdoor bathroom—and it burned right up to the porch here. It's lucky for me it burned out. A-tryin' to burn me out.

Then one day I come in and laying over there on the far side of the railroad tracks was some dynamite. They was going to dynamite the railroad out here in front of my house just to scare me away. But it was wet or something, it went out. I've really had it on this riverbank.

In the mid-sixties, the black lung movement became a major issue in Southern Appalachia. While coal operators were denying the existence of the disease, hundreds of coal miners suffering from black lung and widows whose husbands had died from it were testifying before crowds of coal mining families and the curious news media about the effects of the disease. Finally, in 1969, Congress voted to begin paying compensation to men who had the disease and to the widows of men who had died from black lung. Although the compensation could never pay for the lives of the dead men, the move by the federal government to compensate the widows was significant. It marked the first time that black lung was recognized by this country as a disease which is contracted by an over-accumulation of dust in the coal mines. Granny Hager immediately applied for her black lung benefits.

After Ab passed away in '62, I come up with forty-eight years he'd worked in the mines. In January of '70, I got the form that you fill out to apply for black lung benefits. So I filled out the form. It passed on about two months, they put it on the radio and in the paper—all that had signed up for benefits—the men would have to come to Hazard and *re*-sign. The widow women they'd call in later to the Social Security office to *re*-fill out their forms.

So I go down and I do that. They wanted to know about the death certificate. Well, I thought, then I goes to the funeral home. And the funeral director, he fills out a card for me and I send it in. When it comes back from the Social Security it comes back that Ab died of "general hardening of the arteries."

Then the Social Security called me back in. "You've got nothing to go on, Mrs. Hager. So you's as well as forget about it. You'll not hear from us no more."

I come back home and I was studying what to do next. Then I got another notice to come back in. I went back in and they said, "Mrs. Hager, you'll have to come up with your husband's work record."

I said, "I can come up with nineteen years and a half that he worked at Alloi's, at Columbus Mining Company."

"Columbus Mining Company don't exist," they said. "We can't find it."

I knew it was a lie because back a mile and a half below town those mines worked for about forty years. Right near there they had a Columbus Mining Company.

So I went over to Columbus Mining Company, where it used to be, to Floyd Hurst and he give me Ab's work record, put it down year, month, and all that he worked. Well, I take that back to the Social Security. Passed on a right smart bit I never heard from them.

Then they called me back in again. They said, "We found out Columbus Mining Company *do* exist, but you've got to get the signatures of two or three men that worked with him."

I went over to Reverend Charley down in Wiley Cove. He put down that he pulled coal with Ab for fifteen years or more. I went to another man and he put it down that he chalk-eyed for Ab in the mines for ten years or more. That's where, like a man has a great big place in the mines with different rooms and they hire these men to load the coal for them. They call it chalk-eyeing. Then I went to the man that weighed the coal when it come out to the tipple. So he put it down that he weighed coal for Ab for twenty-five years or more at Columbus Mining Company, Number Four, at Alloi's. And he even put Ab's check number down.

Well, it went and it went and I didn't hear from it. So then I got another letter out of the post office to come in. This time they said, "You're going to have to come up with some doctor's records."

"Doctor Snyder out here doctored him when he got mashed up in the mines," I said. "He's got X-rays but he won't give them to me. He did tell my husband he might live several years if he didn't go back in the mines no more, that his lungs was too bad to go back. And," I said, "he's got the X-rays, but I can't get them."

"Well, people don't keep X-rays."

Then I went to the black lung meeting at Horse Creek. I was supposed to be a witness against Social Security, the way they were a-doin' me. I got over there and when I got up to introduce myself, I didn't know what to say, the first time being on television. We was in a big old basement and there wasn't standing room, there wasn't standing room upstairs and all around that building. Some just couldn't get in hearing hardly of the microphones. So I didn't hardly know what to say.

Well, there was a bunch of pretty good-sized women there. And after I introduced myself I said, "Well, I'll tell you women; if you want to get your schoolgirl figure back, like I got it, you come to Hazard and sign up for something at the Social Security office. And," I said, "when I get through telling you how many trips I made and had to walk it all those miles, you'll understand how *I* got *my* schoolgirl figure back."

I poured it on them pretty heavy. The lawyer asked me did I think it was the fault of the Social Security. "Why are they holding your money up like this, Mrs. Hager?"

I said, "Because the coal operators would rather give them fifty thousand dollars of money to knock me out as to pay what I'd get each month the rest of my life, what time I live. The coal operators is a-payin' the Social Security Board off, for, in nineteen and seventy-three, January the first, the coal operators is going to have to take over and pay. And don't you think the Social Security Board hain't swallering it all, too."

So I talked at the meeting about them—the Social Security Board—and finally they sent a guy out here and he said they'd found all of Ab's X-rays down at the Miners' Hospital. I signed a paper and they took it back. That was on the fourteenth of November, 1970. And then, the seventh of January, 1971, I got my first check.

Now really, I wish something would break in these mountains. I wish something would turn up, or fall out of the sky, or wherever it might come from, that we could wake these mountain people up till they would stand up for their rights and fight for what is honest and just and due them. They's so many of us poor people, I don't care how many big shots there is, if the poor people would stand up, we can run those big shots under the bed.

I've done more work since I got my black lung check than I did before I got it. I have walked in the rain and in the snow ever since I got that check, a-contactin' people about how to get theirs.

Well, I'll tell you, I get awfully bad wore down. I think, well, I'll set down, I won't try no more. But will power keeps me going. And living in hope one or two people will do something about their black lung benefits. I don't get one penny out of it, I don't *want* one penny out of it. The good Lord has made a way that I've got enough to live on now. I never did wear no clothes, but if I got something to eat and can stay warm, that's all I care for.

Well, I'm a-tryin' to put all my time into this, a-tryin' to help the people who have black lung, and the widows. So I don't want no pats on the back, I don't want no reward for it. All I want is for people to get up and move forward and try to help theirselves.

Granny still goes out, slipping between the boxcars, and walks the streets and hollows of Perry County bringing people the news of the Perry County Black Lung Association. She travels all over Southern Appalachia talking to coal miners and widows about their black lung benefits. And, while she is respected and loved by her own people, she is feared by the coal operators, because they know that no obstacle can stand in the way of the legendary Granny Hager.

It's a Hard Life Being a Miner's Wife

DAISY MESSER &
BETTY MESSER SMITH
GOOSE CREEK, KENTUCKY

In the dark outside my window
I can see their carbides shine,
From the graveyard the souls of miners
Walk with my husband to the mine.

The mountain hollows of Eastern Kentucky, like many other areas of Southern Appalachia, were originally part of the American frontier. The first settlers, faced with the problems of survival in an often mean and hostile environment, developed an intense loyalty to the neighbors and kinfolk on whom they depended for mutual help in hard times.

As generations passed on, the original large tracts of land were divided among children and grandchildren, most of whom settled on the land within easy travel of their other kin.

Over the years, the original pioneer families grew to where it was not unusual to find a hundred families with the same name in a county, all of them related in one way or another.

The kinship bonds among these families were honored and respected. So strong was the sense of family loyalty that any wrong inflicted on one member of the kin was bound to be avenged by their family. The famous so-called "feuds"—more accurately called "wars" by people in the mountains—were an outgrowth of the fierce tradition of kinship in mountain counties.

On Goose Creek in Clay County, Kentucky, there is hardly a family that is not either a Jackson, a Smith, or a Messer.

DAISY: When I was just about twelve I remember a whole lot of miners were killed from gas in the mines. And there was a song wrote about them. It was made up from the things they wrote on the walls of the mine before they died. One of the notes said: "Shut up in the mines of Coal Creek." And that was a real lonesome song.

Now, you really feel it. I remember when Robert worked in Harlan for a year. I had six of the children by then. Robert had to stay up there in Harlan and I stayed at home with the children. At night I was scared to death. Well, I loaded my shotgun and set it by my bed. But I always was afraid more for Robert than I was for me.

Robert had his back hurt in the mines. A cross timber fell on him. The men have to crawl in between those timbers and Robert's pretty big, there isn't much space. He would always tell me what went on in the mines. He come home one night and told me about the men being scared when the mine was about to fall in. Well, he was so tired from the escape he didn't remember anything. I told him what he said happened. He said, "I didn't say that!" But while he was asleep he called out, "Look out, it's falling!" But he was so tired from it he didn't remember the slate falling in on them. It made him real nervous. He didn't want to talk about it. Robert usually laughed at things when he'd feel like crying.

It's a bad life being a miner's wife. It's bad for everybody in the family. When you're setting at home, waiting on him to come back to you, and not knowing if he'll make it, you feel like you're in a grave.

BETTY: I can't remember when my daddy first went to work in the mines but he was still working there when I was in high school. I can remember when I was a little kid, Daddy would leave for the mines in the day and he'd always bring us small kids something home like candy, Moon Pies, chewing gum, and then we all divided it.

And I can remember real well the times he got hurt in the mines. They were small hurts but he was still hurt. He'd come in and tell us what'd happened with the dirt and rocks falling on them in the mines. But he was real alert and real lucky and he always escaped. If my man was a miner, I'd be just as scared as Mama was when Daddy went to work in the mines. When he goes in of a morning you don't never know if he'll come out.

Although Betty is a quiet person, she is very outspoken when it comes to talking about the injustices suffered by the poor people around Goose Creek. She and her husband, Junior, along with her mother, Daisy, and the rest of the Messer family have been active in the numerous political battles of poor and working families in Clay County.

There are three families here that control the jobs in this county. They won't bring industry in here because they're afraid of losing their control. If industry came in here people could be independent, but that's what they don't want. They want people to "look up to them" for what they need. But they don't have as much power as they think they have.

Now people like this one woman, who works for the poverty program, she looks down on the people up here, but the people don't look up to her. She came up here to attend a Head Start parents' meeting over at the community center. She always dresses real fine and fancy. Well, when she come in, some of the women from Goose Creek noticed her dress. So one of the women said, "I like your dress." Well, she said, "Thank you. It's the cheapest dress I've got. It only cost me eight dollars."

That didn't go over too big up here. And I know they felt pretty low because some of the women were wearing clothes that was used clothing people had donated to the community. Some of their clothes had cost them fifteen, twenty cents. The women really feel cheated when they're around a woman like that. And inside they resent her very much. But they won't come out with it because they're afraid their welfare money will be taken.

Most of the young people here feel angry that the rich people here have took away their educations. This fight with the poverty program, it's just another thing they're trying to take away from us like they done so many times before, like they took our educations.

The kids from the rich families in Clay County don't date the poor kids. Their parents won't let them associate with poor kids. The rich boys marry the rich girls. The parents of the rich kids don't care anything about them anyway, and I can imagine how it would be if they came home and told their parents they were dating somebody from up in the hollow that didn't have much of anything. And some of the rich guys might try to give the poor girls trouble, take them out to see what they can get out of them.

Some of the kids around here when they see rich kids at school they think, "Well, should we speak to them, should we wave, or should we just act like we don't see them?" Because they're afraid of what the reaction will be; maybe they'll smart off or maybe they won't answer back at all. Some of the kids say, "Well, it's just another fight and the rich guy always comes out on top." And they don't like to think about what's happening cause they don't think they can do anything.

But not with me. With me that won't work. If they don't want to associate with me then I don't want to fool with them. I can act like them if I want to just pretend, but I don't want to. But I could never be like them. I haven't never really associated with rich kids.

John Wears a Gun
When He Goes to the Mines

KATHERINE TILLER

TRAMMEL, VIRGINIA

> *The winter it is cold and lonesome,*
> *The snow drifts in beside the door,*
> *Behind the house that slag heap's burning*
> *Like the fires of Hell forever more.*

Trammel, Virginia, looks like a Monopoly board after the players have finished their game. The narrow highway which forms the center of town is lined on both sides by rows of identical houses. Farther up the side of the mountain there are a few somewhat larger houses backed against the scars the strip miners have left at the top of the ridge.

But there are no Grand Hotels, no Park Places or Broadways in Trammel. Because Trammel represents the game of monopoly as it is played in real life, American free-enterprise style. And the winners in the game, the directors and the shareholders in the mammoth Pittston Company—the same people who brought us the Buffalo Creek disaster in 1972 in which 125 died—which owns the Clinchfield Coal Company mines around Trammel, are not about to make their homes in the narrow, soot-filled valley town with acid polluted streams instead of sidewalks and strip-mined hills for backyards.

Trammel is a census-taker's paradise—everyone in town is an employee of Clinchfield Coal Company. More accurately, if you don't work for the Company you don't stay in Trammel. The houses, the squat company store building, the church are all as much the property of Clinchfield Coal as the coal which is daily dug out of Moss ⚒3, the Company's newest mine twenty miles from town. Almost any family that decides to buck the Company finds itself job hunting and house hunting the same day.

Perhaps the only exception to this rule in Trammel is the Tiller family. They have stayed on in their house halfway up the hill because John Tiller, a foreman at Moss ⚒3, knows how to get coal out of the ground better than almost any other man alive; and because the men who run Clinchfield Coal are justifiably fearful of the consequences of trying to fight folks who have already stood up to them and others in so many battles.

Katherine Tiller's house stands by itself on the mountainside overlooking the town. The place she lives is in itself a symbol of her relationship to the rest of the community. She is at the same time respected for her courage and feared because of the dangers which her outspokenness represents in a tightly run company town. Raised up in coal camps like Trammel, she is at the same time a part of this community and culture and isolated from it. She is accepted and rejected, avoided and sought out, looked down on and looked up to.

The loneliest hours for Katherine are during her husband's shift at the mines. When John is on the day shift and her children are in school, she often sits and reads. Perhaps she has read from the Book of Psalms where it says, "A woman of valor, who can find?" Katherine Tiller is a woman of valor.

I was born in the coal camp in nineteen and twenty-six, a little coal mining camp in McDowell County, West Virginia, called Isaban.

The whole time I was growing up, the men was getting about three days a week in the mines. Mom, she raised a big garden and we ate potatoes, fried potatoes, or fried sweet potatoes for almost every meal. We used scrip in those days. You could get five or maybe even ten dollars' credit at the company store.

I started working at the company store when I started to high school. I had two dresses that my grandmother had made me. They was both print dresses. Thinking back on it now, they was both summer dresses, but I didn't realize that and I wore one or the other every day.

Well, I graduated from high school in May, met John in October, and married him in December. We lived right on the border of McDowell and Mingo counties. John was working in the mines and the children were arriving fast and furious.

Then, in '58, the recession hit and John just couldn't beg, borrow, nor steal a job. We were out of work for about ten months. John tried everywhere to get a job but he just couldn't find one. We lived on his unemployment and there was days when we just did survive.

John got to the point where he'd rather die than go down to the unemployment office and draw that unemployment—and he was due that, he paid into it. John took on his own self, as his own guilt, that he wasn't working, that there was something wrong with him, that he was a failure when it really was the failure of the system.

Our relatives that got food commodities, they would divide them up with us. There was these beans, and they were red, and they were about an inch long. You could soak those beans all night long, and you could cook them all day long as hard as you could cook them . . . and they'd still sound like rocks when they hit your plate. I didn't even want to go visit our relatives cause I felt like they were thinking, "Here she comes with all those kids, after a meal."

Then John got a job in a small mine—it was a hot mine—there was so much gas it was terrible. So he come in one night and said, "I just can't take it any more. I quit." I began to get a little bit of my self-respect back then.

When John quit the small mine he told me, "Don't worry." There was a company, Clinchfield Coal Company, opening a huge operation over in Virginia. John said to me, "Don't worry, because tomorrow I'm going to Virginia and when I come back I'm going to have a job." And, you know, he did.

When we were living in Ragland, West Virginia, where John had a job for a while, we had to pay for our water. We had been cut off work about three months, and one day we hadn't paid our water bill for that month. This man came up to the door and he wanted two-fifty or he was going to cut off the water. I begged him, I told him just as soon as we got our paycheck we'd pay him. He just said no, and he cut it off.

I got so mad. I got wild. My whole body got numb. It

affected my hands and my eyes and it lasted a long time. I must have been about six months pregnant at the time. I kind of date my trouble with the baby back to that time. That's why he was born premature, why he wasn't strong enough, why he couldn't make it.

He was such a beautiful baby, such a fat little baby, with bright red hair. And we took him home. The next morning, the baby began to make strange little noises and bring his little arms up in the air and his little mouth would draw up. When Mama saw him she said to take him back to the hospital. So we took him back. I knew then the baby wasn't going to make it. And he didn't. His lungs collapsed.

I was so hurt. He was like a ray of sunshine to the family. Our oldest boys, Johnny and Mark, they'd even named him after a Cincinnati baseball player, a Black man named George Crow. But of course we called him Kevin. He was such a lovely baby, after he was born John felt like everything was going to be just fine from then on. Then to have him snatched away from us like that . . . We didn't have any money. And people that says money don't matter is dead wrong, cause when you don't have it, it does matter.

The death of children is sadly an important part of life in the Southern Appalachian Mountains. Many who have written about Southern Appalachia have commented on what appears to be the fatalism of the people and have suggested that this is perhaps a reaction to the high mortality not only of children but of people of all ages. In fact, this is not fatalism but a realistic understanding of things as they are.

Death is so much a part of life for people like Katherine Tiller, not because of any mystical or fatalistic beliefs, but because of the persistent lack of nourishing food, of adequate medical care, of health facilities that exists almost everywhere in Southern Appalachia.

For a long time the women of Southern Appalachia have had one of the highest birth rates in the nation. At the same time, the fatality rate for children is among the highest anywhere in the United States. Many families have reacted to this overabundance of death with what has been interpreted by outsiders as fatalism. They have reacted sometimes with bitterness, sometimes by turning to religion. For others, tragedy, whether the death of young children or the death of husbands or fathers in the mines, has served to push them in other directions. For them, perhaps not immediately, but after a while, the response has been anger, disbelief that such things must happen, and finally determination to change the way things are.

I guess what really made me political was that our oldest boy, Johnny, was going to be drafted, and I began trying to find something wrong about the war in Viet Nam. I felt kind of cheap for a long time because, to be frank, I didn't want Johnny in danger. But more than that, I didn't want him to kill people, kill people en masse . . . just slaughter people. *I* had no quarrel with the Vietnamese. . .

When Johnny got his induction notice, we were desperate, we were afraid. We didn't have any advice, anybody to talk to. All the information we had was what we saw on the television and read in the magazines. We had no one to contact, we knew no organizations. Johnny was to report to the Army on a Tuesday. He left for Canada the Sunday before.

Then the time came for Mark to go. Mark is a very nonviolent person. I always had the feeling Mark wanted to go to jail as a form of protest, just to refuse induction. But my feeling was, it's no protest if no one knows, and who's going to know? They just shut them off in prison, you can't do anything there, and how's anyone going to know?

Mark received two notices to appear for a physical, which he ignored. Finally he went to Canada. He didn't emigrate right off, though. When Mark left, he told me, "No matter what, I'm coming back to Washington for the Peace March at the Pentagon in October. No matter what." And he came back to Washington in October and he was at the demonstration and he was arrested. He was in jail for eleven days there. Then he came home for a few months.

While Mark was at home, the FBI came one day. The man told him, "Mark, I hope you think a long time before you take the step your brother did." Mark kindly grinned and said, "I've a feeling you're going to be here asking my mom questions about *me* one of these days."

Well then, Martin Luther King was assassinated and Mark left for Canada on the day he was buried. He got there safely and he emigrated.

Mountain people leave their homes only out of necessity. Sometimes it is to find a job, and sometimes the emotional and physical strain of hard luck and hard labor forces a hillbilly to seek a new life outside the mountains. Katherine Tiller's children left home out of moral necessity.

At first, Katherine's neighbors were horrified at the Tiller family's stand of nonviolence. Soon after her sons went to Canada, Katherine found herself alienated from the other women in the community. Although they would speak to her, they rarely mentioned her sons, and it was not long before the people in the coal camp branded the Tillers as "radicals." Rumors flew through the coal camp about John draft counseling young coal miners at the mines. The Tillers began to realize their courage would soon be tested.

Well, these threats had been coming to us for a while. Men John works in the mines with were telling him, "Well, John, I heard down at the courthouse, I heard them say they're going to run you out of the county one way or the other—if they can't run you out one way, they'll run you out in a box."

With all the threats that had been made against John, I knew and feared what was to come. Course Larry was only an excuse. He was from here and he was Black.

Larry had gone off to Detroit and had got hung up on dope. In December of '69, he come to our house and asked if he could stay here till he got his head together. He couldn't afford to keep his habit up. So I just said stay here and tried to get him to go back to school.

One night while Larry was staying here, he and three of my children rode the school bus to the high school basketball game. During halftime, the deputy sheriff called Larry out and said to him, "We don't like niggers staying with White folks and you better get out of Tiller's house, get out of the Grove. Better still, go on, get out of the county." Then he asked Larry about his draft status. So Larry said he'd come home to register for the draft. Well, the deputy said, he'd be checking to see that he did.

On the way back home from the game, a few big guys in the back of the bus, they threatened Larry. The bus driver, he cut the lights off, which he wasn't supposed to do on night trips. But they never did do nothing to Larry on the bus except threaten him. When the children came home they told me what had happened.

I didn't tell Larry and my children how frightened I was that night. John was off at the mines and wouldn't be back till three in the morning. I felt sure they was coming to get Larry. We later found out that twenty-five or thirty of them had a meeting that night and was planning on coming up here and getting Larry. They was planning to take him out and hang him. We still don't know why they didn't come. I sat up all night with a loaded .22 waiting for them to come. And when John come in I told him what had happened.

The next afternoon, John left for the mines. He rode to work with the deputy's brother and the deputy's son, who he usually rode with. When he got in the car, John saw they had a rifle, a gun, and two fifths of whiskey. So he asked them about that. They gave him a reasonable answer: they might come up on a rabbit or a ground hog. Well, that wasn't unusual—they shoot them just to kill something.

When the car got to the top of the mountain, John saw the deputy's car parked at the turn, kind of dropped off into the hill. A bright winter sun blinded him as they got near to the car. Then the car John was riding in stopped. And all of a sudden there was the deputy, standing there with a gun in his hand.

The deputy came over to the car and opened the door where John was sitting. Then he knocked John's glasses off. He took hold of the barrel of the gun and started beating John with the butt end. The deputy was all that was beating him, but the other two just sat there and didn't do a thing to help him.

The deputy was shouting, "You gotta learn! You gotta stay away from those goddamned niggers, you gotta stay away from those goddamned draft dodgers! I'm gonna kill you . . ." It was rage.

By that time the blood was just pouring. Then the deputy backed off, pointing the gun straight at John. Suddenly John realized the other two had a-hold of the deputy, holding him back and saying, "Not now! Let's get outa here, let's get outa here!" At the same time it registered on John that in the distance a car was coming. They didn't want any witnesses . . . so they got in their cars and drove off.

Well, John went on to the mines, went in to the bathroom, washed up, and started work. But then he knew they'd try to finish him off on the way back home. And he was starting to realize he'd been hurt a lot worse than he thought. So he got one of the men to bring him home early. That was a year ago, and since then John wears a gun when he goes to the mines.

I'm not afraid. The only thing that would worry me is if Johnny and Mark ever tried to come back here. When we go to visit them, the people here in the camp get real upset because the government allows us to go see them. But then it sort of wears off and people get trustful again and we feel like we're just one of them . . . until the next time we go to Canada. But I'm sure that sooner or later . . . well, even the people here don't see no sense in the war. Some of them has lost their children in it.

I'm not afraid any more.

Someday Us Poor
Is Going to Overrule

SHIRLEY DALTON
DELLSLOW, WEST VIRGINIA

You give me your old dresses that you never worked to earn
And you think that if it weren't for you I'd have no place to turn,
But the thing that keeps me going through the hard times that we're
in
Is the pride that comes from knowing who I am and where I've
been.

Morgantown is the intellectual hub of West Virginia. Its steep
hills are the home of West Virginia University, the academic
pride of the Mountaineer State. Even poverty has been good
to West Virginia University; out of its tax-supported halls
have come dozens of government-financed studies about poor
people and their problems, some of them as thick as the State
welfare manual.

All of this intellectual "progress" has brought problems to
Morgantown, including some of the worst traffic jams this

66

side of the New Jersey turnpike. To deal with this crisis the town has applied for and received a $36 million grant to construct the first monorail system in the Eastern United States. The system is completed now, and tourists and townspeople have fast and efficient transportation at their disposal. But you can bet your last token Shirley Dalton is still walking to town.

There are no monorail stations in Dellslow, West Virginia, an unincorporated community three miles from the University gates where Shirley lives. For that matter there are no sidewalks, no sewer lines, no water pipes, no libraries, no medical clinics. The nearest thing to a public facility in Dellslow is the three-room house where Shirley Dalton lives with her husband Darris and their seven children. In the evenings, after the work is done, the working people who make up Dellslow's population come by Shirley's house to talk things over.

Their children will not go to West Virginia University unless it is as janitors and cafeteria cooks; they will get their education as coal miners or housewives trying to raise families in tarpaper shacks, the dormitories in which poor children are forced to live while society teaches them their place.

Shirley Dalton is an educated woman. She knows things that the professors at West Virginia University with their subsidized salaries and federally sponsored studies of the poor will never understand. She knows what it is to be poor and powerless, to be poor and pushed around, to be poor and political, to be poor and proud. She is all these things and she is not ashamed of any of them.

The motto of the state of West Virginia is, "Mountaineers are always free." Shirley Dalton is one West Virginian who lives up to it.

It's always been there was trouble for us. We've fought from day to day, know what I mean? From day to day we've fought, worrying about where the next meal's coming from.

When I was on welfare I drawed a hundred and eighty-two dollars a month. Out of that I got food stamps for fifty-six dollars. And my doctor bills was being paid and my hospital and medicine I need on account of I'm an epileptic. My Dylantin pills I gotta have the rest of my life.

Okay. On welfare I didn't have to worry about that. But now, since Darris has a job—and not making but forty cents over standard pay—I been cut off. And my food stamps got raised and they took my medical card away. So what am I supposed to do?

When my kids get sick, I don't take them to the hospital. I can't. I've been there and I know what the place is. They don't want you if you've not got the money to lay right there in their hands. They turn you away.

It's like this: our tax money that we buy pop with is a-payin' for it, right? All right. When we go there, if we're on welfare, why do they shun us? I seen a guy lay there in an epileptic for two hours and they never laid a hand on him.

I took my daughter over there to the hospital. She got hurt in school. They had to call a special doctor down to the hospital. The ligaments in her leg was all pulled. Her leg completely twisted. The doctor came over there and jerked on that leg. She give out a scream. Well, he slammed her leg down and he said to me, "You take her home. She's a bawl baby and I ain't gonna work on her." And he didn't. He slammed her leg down and pushed her out.

There's three rooms in this house. With nine of us living here it's not that peaceful. Until last summer we lived in two rooms, the nine of us. My kids has to sleep on the floor right there in front of the coal fire. It's not that safe with all that bedding so close up to the fire. You gotta do with what you got, you know? People can look and they can say you don't try to do nothing. But how are you *supposed* to?

There was one time when my husband went to work for the OEO. He worked on the roads with some other men. Well, they never did get their paychecks. They couldn't even afford to buy the gas to drive to work. Well, the OEO man he told them one day, "If you all don't show up for work tomorrow, you're all fired." But the men couldn't get there. And every one of them was fired.

We went one month without no help of any kind. We had no coal. We had nothing. No gas nor nothing to cook with. We didn't have nothing to eat anyhow.

I went into Morgantown and I asked the welfare for coal. They wouldn't give it to me. They gave me a seven-dollar food stamp for the nine of us. Now, that's what we lived off for one month. I had one loaf of bread to divide up between the nine of us. We chopped wood to keep a fire going. The worst part was having to see the kids go hungry. *Oh no*, and don't they say people in this country don't starve! *They* ain't never seen the day come.

After the OEO fired all the men, a caseworker came up

here. She said why didn't I put my husband in jail. Because he wasn't working. It didn't bother *me* so bad, but she said it in front of the kids. And a kid understands.

Now, I have a boy that's fourteen. And he don't want to go to school. He's afraid. He's been knocked down, hit in the head, his clothes were torn off him, and the cook at the schoolhouse knocked his legs out from under him, him with his tray—put a knot in his head. He don't want to go to school, he'll do anything to stay at home.

Now a boy's a boy, I don't care who they are. They're gonna be bad. But that don't mean the teacher's gotta beat him. There's gonna be a court against the teachers here. Eighty children was beaten in one school. Some of those kids aren't even in the fourth grade out there.

Now. They get a lunch ticket. The teacher told my boy if he loses his lunch ticket once more, he gets no more. Now, I can't afford to pay for their lunches. For four days he went without lunch and I never knew it. He'd lost his ticket and was afraid to ask for it. And he's got pride.

I don't want my kids to be ashamed. When they got to live on welfare they gotta live on it. But they ought not to be ashamed over it. I try to show them not to be ashamed, that it ain't no sin. I'd rather see them eating than to see them have false pride.

I can see it in the stores. People is ashamed they get food stamps. Their faces is as red as a beet. But I can't see being ashamed. Because before I'm going to let my kids go hungry, *I'm* gonna *fight*. I'm gonna be at that welfare department and I'm gonna be there till I get something. Darris has worked hard all his life too, and he's paid into it. We're due that help.

Anyway, I'm proud to be poor. I'm glad I hain't got

anything anybody else has got. These rich people that's got all the money, they don't know what it is to have a hurt. But when that hurt hurts them, nobody will look at them and say, "You helped me when I was out. Now it's my turn to help you." Nobody will be there.

Your Bible tells you, "Earn your bread by the sweat of your brow." Right? Okay, now. No matter what you do, if it's the *right* thing, you're going to be working hard. You're not a communist, you're just fighting for your rights.

Shirley Dalton is fighting for her rights, and for the rights of other poor people in the state of West Virginia. Ever since the time Shirley was forced to draw welfare money she has been trying to make a change in the state welfare system. She has organized rallies and protests and has spoken to U. S. Senator Edward Kennedy about the national welfare programs. She is a member of the National Welfare Rights Organization, was a delegate to the 1972 state democratic convention, and has helped organize antiwar protests.

Shirley's platform is a guaranteed annual income. She believes it is the right of every human being to have enough to eat, decent housing, clothes to wear, and proper medical attention. She knows from her own experience what it is like to go without these things.

Where in the name of God is all our church people at today? These big, beautiful churches they're a-buildin' . . . that ain't gonna get them to heaven. But when it comes to the poor, their *own living brother* . . . and then they can stand up in that pulpit and preach.

Well, we don't know when our time's a-gonna come.

Now, I may not have fifty cents, but for a dying child, God, I'd be willing to give it. If they'd read their Bible: "Love thy neighbor as thyself. Do unto others as you would have them do unto you." Now, who's a-doin' it to-day?

I've got a lot of burdens, too. But I'm supposed to have. But, my God in heaven, if I have to take my last penny out of my Dylantin pills money I'm gonna do it to help this boy up here who's dying and needs a kidney machine. A dollar ain't gonna hurt nobody. God knows who got it and who don't.

How many people's gonna die and leave here feeling this on their mind? Not these rich people. They're putting their money away to put them through heaven. But they're gonna be burning right in hell with the rest of us.

I'm Pentecostal all the way around. Now, my church is just a little old country church, but I'm proud of it. The people there will speak to you. But where Commissioner Flowers goes to church—he's the State Welfare Director —I went there one time. Hey, listen, I'm gonna tell you . . . they took holy communion! Now, my Bible tells me you don't take it unless you're pure.

Okay, I felt bad. It was one of them big fancy churches. I walked in, all these people had on these fancy clothes and fancy hats. And I was in my old Sunday clothes. I knowed they all looked at me. But I felt this way, buddy. God give them clothes to me. If He didn't want me to wear them, He wouldn't have gave them to me. And I'm not going to set down and beg for something I don't need.

No, sir, I didn't take holy communion—uh-uh. I'm not pure enough. They passed it around, Commissioner Flowers took it. Then they stand up and tell this thing: "The poor of this world needs help." Yeah. The poor needs help, but *who's gonna help them?* Is Commissioner Flowers gonna help them? He better pray a little bit more, read his Bible.

I've only been in old-time churches. I didn't even know I was in a church. We was invited to hear some "literature about poor people." And when we got there it was services.

I don't believe in a church that thinks they're bigger than somebody else. Where all the people go dressed up and they think they gotta have a new dress every Sunday. No, I don't believe in that. And an old man that sits back in the corner with raggedy clothes and nobody speaks to him. That's not God's work.

I cuss and I smoke. But I will never lose my faith. Your Bible tells you, it ain't what goes in you, it's what comes out of you. It kind of makes me wonder sometimes.

One night the baby had got Kool-Aid and was nearly choked to death. I thought she was just choking a little bit, so I picked her up and shook her and it got worse. So I called to Darris and he come out and picked her up. Her head was back on his shoulder, her eyes were up in her head till you could only see the whites. And I thought, my God, there's no use to run. I had nowhere to run to. And I thought she was dead.

Then something said to me, "Believe in God and say a prayer. Put your hand up on her head in the name of God." I put my hand on her and said a prayer and she was all of a sudden all right. I almost went to talking in tongues.

I took Pauline, one of my girls, over there to the tent meeting and had her prayed for, and she throwed her brace away. She didn't need it no more.

Yeah, God knows what it is to suffer. No food to eat, no clothes for the kids to wear to school, no coats to wear, no boots for their feet. Nobody could tell it unless they been through it.

Jesus helped the poor. And He *was* poor. When the Poor Man died, he went to heaven. When the rich man died, he went to hell. So I don't want to be rich. I want to get to heaven someday. If you was to say that in some of these big churches they'd laugh.

My epilepsy pills is about to run out now. I don't know how I'm gonna get some more. Darris drawed seventy-two dollars this last paycheck. We had fifty cents left after we paid our bills.

The time will come. *Someday us poor is going to over-rule.* We're gonna do it, by the help of God we're gonna do it. I believe it. I honest to God do. The poor is going to overrule. I've got faith in that.

You get discouraged fighting for your rights. But if you didn't get discouraged once in a while, why would you work? It's gotta be a way of stopping us from saying we won't fight no more. If everything in the world was right, there wouldn't be no need for a heaven, you see.

You got to shine a little light to let people know who you are.

It Was Me and Jack
That Stopped the Train

DELLA MAE SMITH

RODELLE, WEST VIRGINIA

But I'm proud to be a hillbilly woman,
The kind of working girl that built this mountain land,
Yes, I'll live and die a hillbilly woman,
Work side by side with my Blue Ridge mountain man.

All over the Southern mountains there are families who are victims of foreign wars. Hillbilly women have been widowed by battles in Normandy, Guadalcanal, Korea, and Vietnam. Others have welcomed home husbands disabled by the savagery of modern warfare, men who have lost arms, legs, faces, eyes in this country's wars.

If the number of maimed and crippled men in the mountains is startling, it is not only the result of the terrible tool exacted by this country's wars which are fought by hillbillies

75

and other American minority groups. It is also the result of a struggle on their home front.

Della Mae Smith's husband, Jack, is a victim of this kind of war, a victim of the battle for survival in the mountains. As a result of a coal mining accident, Jack has spent most of his married life in a wheelchair.

Through it all Della Mae has stayed with him and the only thing they have asked from other people is that they be as angry as they are at what has happened to so many coal miners in the Southern mountains.

In the picture album Della Mae keeps in her house in Rodelle, West Virginia, there are pictures of the two of them surrounded by their four children. They are strong, handsome people; their solidness, their humor, their warmth all come through in the photographs almost as well as they do when you meet them. But they are angry, too, and their anger has led them to fight as hard for the rights of their friends and neighbors as they have for themselves.

In 1970, when Della Mae and Jack joined other disabled miners, miners' wives and widows in support of the coal miners' strike, someone tried to start a rumor that Jack had been attacked by company men. If the story was believed in other places it got nowhere in the coal camps around Rodelle. People there know that no one in his right mind tries to cross Jack and Della Mae Smith, anywhere, any time.

Jack lost his legs from a slate fall in the mines. That was in October of 1953. He went to work in the mines on the twelfth of October, 1952, and got hurt a year later. A year to the day.

We'd been married about a year and a half when it happened, but some people, when they talk about it, they tell it like we had only been married a few weeks or a few days. I guess they think it makes a better story that way.

The day Jack got hurt, I was at mother's and a friend of Jack's that worked with him in the mines come over and told me he was at the Miners' Hospital. And he took me down there to see Jack.

His back was busted six inches and then broke. It was a big piece of coal rock hit him all the way down. He was hit on the top of the head and on the shoulder. Broke the shoulder three times, busted his legs, killed all the nerves in the spine.

Me and an orderly washed him, then they transferred him to Bluefield. He stayed there eight weeks. Then they sent him to Washington, D.C. I think they used him for a guinea pig in Washington, D.C., but he never did question them. He had twenty-three operations and it never bothered him.

Jack stayed in the hospital in Washington for thirteen months and nine days. United Mine Workers Union sent him to George Washington University Hospital there. He still had his legs, but he was paralyzed from the waist down.

In Washington they were trying to rehabilitate him. To learn him to walk. Then he came home. But he never did walk again.

Jack was given up to die three times. One time, he took poison in his legs and they said twenty-four hours was the lifetime for him.

It was June the sixth, 1956, they took the first leg off. Then they took the other one off July the eleventh of '56. At that time he weighed about ninety-eight pounds soaking wet.

When the doctor told me down there at Mullins that

they'd have to take his legs off—I'm like him, I never give up him walking again as long as he had his legs—it like to killed me. The doctor said, "You want me to tell him?" I says yes. He went upstairs and told him. Jack didn't pay it no mind. It didn't seem to bother him.

I thought when he realized what was going to happen to him, losing his legs, he'd break up. But he came out of that operating room like he'd been to a party. He never did pay it no mind.

When Jack got hurt, it took two months to get his workmen's compensation started. He got about sixty dollars every two weeks. Then after they took his legs off they finally awarded him total disability. But he never got no lump sum. He never got no payment for his legs.

Jack joined the United Mine Workers Union right as soon as he went to work in the mines. He got to keep his union health card four years after he got hurt. Then they took it. They say John L. Lewis did that before he got out. Made it so that if a man got hurt, they took his card after four years.

We lived on workmen's compensation until we started getting welfare in 1956. Now we get twenty-four dollars a month for me and Jack. The kids, they get eight dollars and sixty cents for the four of them. That's two dollars and some a month each.

We have meetings of the disabled miners here in Rodelle twice a week. We're fighting to get our hospital cards back from the union. But the union never has done us no good. And the coal companies have threatened to fire the active miners if they come to our meetings.

In 1970, when the disabled miners first went out on strike

with the active miners, Jack was out there in his wheelchair on the picket line. The disabled miners was out to get their hospital cards and their pensions. I asked Jack to let me go with him. He said no, it's no place for a woman. Then when the other women started going, well, he let me go down. So then me and him went together.

During the strike there was a rumor that got out. It wasn't true. One of the miners told the strikers that Jack had been pushed over the hill into the creek in his wheelchair. He told it to make the miners angry, to get them mad. They use the fact that Jack lost his legs in the mines to get the men mad. But the people shouldn't need that to make them angry. And me and Jack don't like it.

During the strike, Jack would get up at five o'clock in the morning, go up there to East Gulf Mining Company, and he wouldn't get back from the picket line until seven of a evening. Sometimes they'd drive straight over to another mine and picket the night shift. But we still didn't get nothing from the union out of helping the miners to picket.

Tony Boyle was the UMW President then and he wouldn't do nothing for nobody. The union should have pulled the active miners out of the mines when the contract ran out for the disabled miners. Active miners, they benefit from the strikes, but the disabled miners and the widows they never get nothing.

Tony Boyle followed John L. Lewis in the leadership of the United Mine Workers Union. Considered one of Lewis' "wonder boys," Boyle built the UMW into one of the most corrupt and scandal-ridden labor unions in America.

During the numerous strikes of coal miners under Boyle's leadership, the UMW was successful in raising the wages of union coal miners but virtually ignored non-union miners, disabled miners, and widows of men who died in mine disasters. Often, Boyle would appoint his staff members as rewards for political favors rather than by competence.

Shortly after the 1969 elections for UMW officers, in which Boyle was reinstated as President of the UMW, Jock Yablonski, Boyle's opponent in the election, and his wife and daughter were murdered in their home while they slept. Following that, Boyle was arrested and indicted for making illegal campaign contributions with almost $50,000 of UMW funds. He was tried and convicted of the charge and is at this writing out of jail on bail and appealing his conviction.

The mechanics of the UMW became so corrupt that a group of miners from Kentucky and West Virginia organized an insurgent group called the Miners For Democracy and in the 1972 election they ran a disabled coal miner from West Virginia, Arnold Miller, against Boyle. In a government-supervised election, Miller ousted Boyle. Miller, "the people's candidate," has promised to clean house at the UMW headquarters. For men like Jack Smith and women like Granny Hager, who campaigned for Miller, it was indeed a people's victory.

It was me and Jack that stopped the train during the strike. We didn't have a twelve-gauge shotgun like some folks say. We went out here to the crossing and we heard the train coming through the tunnel. So I said to Jack, "Let's stop this train. If it can't pull no coal," I says, "then we won't have to worry about East Gulf." We had a sign with us that said *Hospital and Pension Card* on it. And we just held it up. We was beside the tracks, over on the edge, we didn't really block the train. But they saw our sign and they stopped the train. They pulled it back into the company's yard.

The state patrols come up to us and said, "As long as you all don't block the crossing, you'll not get no trouble from us." And they went off. The train men parked the train, got out and went to the yard, got in their cars and drove home.

The other disabled miners, they wouldn't go by themselves and stop the train like Jack did. They're scared. Won't none of them go unless they've got fifty or seventy-five men. I told them, "Well, what are you scared of? You all are up and able to run if things get rough. And Jack went right by hisself." I said, "There's nothing to be scared of. If the train men are man enough they'll honor your picket line. What's there to be scared of?" I've went right to the mines to picket by myself and I wasn't scared.

We keep fighting for the union, but so far the disabled miners and widows haven't got nothing for the help we give them every time they go out on strike. If there was a picket line I feel I'd have to go on it. But I won't attend no more meetings with the union people just to hear the same talk I've heard for years. I'm wiser now.

My daddy was a coal miner up until the day Jack got hurt. He went to work that day and the news got to him that Jack was hurt in a slate fall. He asked the boss to let him off to go see Jack. His boss said no, he couldn't get off, so he just walked off. And that's the last day Daddy worked in the mines.

I guess it takes courage to stop a coal train, but you've got to have courage to fight for your rights. A lot of people likes to get up and make long speeches and take big bows for what they're doing a-fightin' for people's rights. I don't like to say what I'm going to do. I like to *do* it.

Part Two

BLUE RIDGE MOUNTAIN REFUGEES

BLUE RIDGE MOUNTAIN REFUGEE

I'm working in a factory and thinking how it feels
To be bringing home good money like my mama never seen,
But a feeling follows after me like a hound dog at my heels,
Cause I know that I'll never see my mountain home again.

    Oh, they say that you can't go home again,
    Never set and talk among your childhood friends,
    Never live among your neighbors and your kin,
    No, you'll never see your mountain home again.

Down at the railway station in the early afternoon,
You can see them carrying bundles that are all done up in twine,
And they hear the whistle from the South, they're saying their
    good-byes,
And they say that they'll be back but they're leaving for all time.

    Don't they know that they can't go home again,
    Never set and talk among their childhood friends,
    Never live among their neighbors and their kin,
    No, they'll never see their mountain homes again.

In Cincinnati, Baltimore, Chicago, and Detroit,
You will find us by the thousands with our husbands and our wives,
If you wonder what we're doing here so far from our mountain
    homes,
We're Blue Ridge Mountain refugees, fighting for our lives.

    And we know that we can't go home again,
    Never set and talk among our childhood friends,
    Never live among our neighbors and our kin,
    No, we'll never see our mountain homes again.

Blue Ridge Mountain Refugees

WYOMING WILSON
MARIE CHANDLER
ARTIE CHANDLER
CINCINNATI, OHIO

In Cincinnati, Baltimore, Chicago, and Detroit,
You will find us by the thousands with our husbands and our wives,
If you wonder what we're doing here so far from our mountain
*   homes,*
We're Blue Ridge Mountain refugees, fighting for our lives.

During the great migration of mountain families after World
War II, thousands of people left their homes in Eastern Kentucky and traveled to Cincinnati, Ohio, looking for jobs. They
settled in "Over the Rhine," Cincinnati's worst slum, and
soon their numbers grew to almost a hundred thousand Blue
Ridge Mountain refugees.

But hillbillies found the city did not offer them what they
had expected. Many could not find jobs, some were turned

down for employment because they were hillbillies. Learning to survive in the city was a harsh new experience for people used to living, if just barely, off the land.

There is nothing good about living in a slum. Nothing pleasant about rat-infested, run-down housing, people crowded into tiny spaces, families of five, six, or seven sharing a two-room flat. For mountain people who are used to open spaces where children can play without fear of being molested, people used to air that is fresh and clean, living in a slum is claustrophobic.

Most mountain people arrive in the city with just enough money to buy their next meal. Whether they find work or are forced onto the welfare rolls, there is never enough money to meet the high cost of living in a city slum. Most hillbilly migrants live from one day to the next. Perhaps the only motivation for making it through the day is the distant hope that one day they will have enough money to take them back home to the country.

Wyoming Wilson was widowed in the fifties, her husband the victim of a mine accident in Eastern Kentucky. Unable to support herself and her six children, since jobs for women are scarce in the Southern mountains, Wyoming migrated to Cincinnati to find a way of survival.

After she found a job, she went back to Kentucky and brought her children, who had been living with their grandmother, to the city. One of those children was Marie Chandler, then a young girl of eleven years, frightened of the city, saddened by leaving the mountains and her playmates behind.

As soon as Marie arrived in Cincinnati, she learned for the first time what it means to be discriminated against. She did not know, however, that her troubles would become worse. Marie spent most of her first year in the city in a hospital, a young girl in a strange place suffering from paralysis and spinal meningitis. But she inherited the strength of her ancestors, her mother and her grandfather, Tom Hicks, and she learned to survive in the hillbilly ghetto.

Just about the time Wyoming was making the trip to Cincinnati, another family, the Chandlers, were traveling the same road. The coal mine in Eastern Kentucky where George Chandler had worked for twenty-seven years shut down, leaving the Chandler family with no choice but to migrate in search of work. Artie and George Chandler brought their son, Bill, with them to the city. Like Marie, Bill learned quickly that Over the Rhine wasn't exactly hillbilly heaven.

These two families went through the hardships and suffering of most hillbillies who are forced to leave their mountain homes. Somehow, Bill and Marie got together, on a fire escape, it seems, and the families were joined by their marriage.

The first time I met Wyoming Wilson and Artie and Marie Wilson Chandler in 1972, I was impressed by the extreme closeness and feeling of kinship among them. Bill and Marie, their three babies, and Artie and George Chandler were all living together in a three-room apartment on the second floor of a run-down building in the heart of Over the Rhine. Wyoming was luckier and had her own apartment; luckier in one sense, but also very much alone.

Wyoming works in a vending machine factory and supports herself. Artie has worked most of her life in various factories and stores. George Chandler worked as a repair man in apartment buildings, despite the fact that he has been disabled with black lung for over twenty years. Bill Chandler works at a youth center called the Appalachian Identity Center on Vine Street in Over the Rhine. It is the only place besides the streets where young hillbillies can get together. It is, in fact, the only safe place in the neighborhood for young people. The kids come into the center every day, read books, watch television, and play pool. If it weren't for the Appalachian Identity Center and Bill Chandler, the problems in Over the Rhine would be much worse than they are now.

Marie Chandler is a housewife and a mother. She takes superb care of her three little girls and keeps up her apartment well. But she doesn't confine herself to the house and the children. Often Marie will go around the corner to the Center and help Bill, or she will visit her mother and her in-laws. About once a week Marie indulges in her one addiction, Bingo.

The Chandler-Wilson family is typical of many hillbilly migrant families and I chose to work with the family as a group because they represent the importance of kinship in the life of a hillbilly migrant.

In Wyoming's chapter, I have spent a lot of time covering the history of her father, Tom Hicks. He is probably one of the most important yet little-known folk heroes of the early struggles in the Eastern Kentucky coal fields. And he had a strong influence on the development of the stamina of his daughter, Wyoming.

Over the Rhine is a horrible place to live if you are a poor hillbilly, but the Wilsons and the Chandlers have made it this far. The strength and courage that they have demonstrated up to now will no doubt be the basis for their survival. But one cannot help but be outraged that problems like theirs and so many other Blue Ridge Mountain refugees are pompously pushed aside by the people who are responsible for these conditions.

There are no mountains in Cincinnati. Someone once suggested that if Cincinnati had mountains hillbilly migrants might feel a whole lot better.

WE NEVER SETTLED IN ONE PLACE
Wyoming Wilson

My dad gave me the name Wyoming. He told me that before he ever married, he left Kentucky and went to Missouri. Well, he was sort of running . . . he was outlawing. So he went to the state of Wyoming and hid out there. He worked on a ranch and they called the ranch Wyoming. When he left there, he started back to the Southern mountains, on his way to Tennessee.

Well, that was during World War I. When he got to Missouri, he picked up the suitcase he'd left there and started off to Tennessee. But on the way he decided to join the Army. So he just dropped his suitcase in the river and went off and joined the Army. He said then the first girl he ever had he'd call her Wyoming.

My father's name was Tom Hicks. He was what they call an organizer. Well, I was born in 1922 in Coxton, Kentucky, during all the trouble they was having in the coal fields. Then in '28 or '29, when the organizing got real strong, Dad moved us to Black Joe in Harlan County, Kentucky.

In the late twenties, union organizing in the Eastern Kentucky coal fields was at its peak. Harlan and Bell counties were the center of most of the organizing being done by the United Mine Workers and the National Miners Union, a new union which had come into Eastern Kentucky to work with the UMW.

In 1931 a strike was called by the NMU and thousands of miners in Bell and Harlan counties went out on strike. Tom Hicks and his brother, Sam, were two of the men on strike.

The coal operators, fearing the strength of the rebellious miners, hired 325 armed guards. Some of the armed guards were deputized and given legal sanction to search houses of families on strike, to arrest any coal miner suspected of "insubordination" to the coal operators, and to shoot and kill any miner they might consider "dangerous."

In April of 1931, one of these armed guards, commonly known as gun thugs, shot and wounded a coal miner. The coal miner shot back and killed the guard.

On the morning of May 5, 1931, the "deputies" attempted to run some of the striking miners off a picket line. But the miners had been tipped off that the thugs were coming and they met them at a railroad crossing. It has been said that during the battle of Evarts a thousand shots were fired.

Florence Reece recalls in her story about the battle of Evarts that a little boy tipped off the miners about the gun thugs. She also recalls that there were eleven men killed during the battle, four of them miners, the rest gun thugs.

When all this murdering and killing happened over at Evarts, that was when the coal company hired gun thugs and they met up with the miners that was out on strike. Well, Dad took the blame for those killings. Course, he'd been a coal miner all his life and they'd worked him day and night in those mines. And he worked with the union to make things better for the people.

But Dad wasn't at Evarts when the killings happened. He was out robbing the commissary. But Dad's brother, Sam Hicks, was there at Evarts. I think he was the one that had the machine gun. But all this time Dad was robbing the company store.

I think it was in the spring of the year, long about '31. Dad and the other miners had come out on strike and the gun thugs was after them.

I remember Dad coming to the house and getting the shotgun and a lot of shells. He made us all get under the floor and told Mommy to keep us barricaded under there and not let us out. And I remember Mom a-beggin' him not to go out. But they had been working him hard in those mines, night and day. So he went out and joined the other miners on strike.

So anyway, this night he come in after the shotgun, that was the night before the killings at Evarts started. But Dad, the reason he wanted the gun was some of the miners and their families was starving and they needed some food. He aimed to get it for them.

Dad went up to the commissary and took about five other men with him. He went into the commissary and held his shotgun on the company men. Then he told the miners to fill all these bags full of food. They filled hundred pound bags of beans, sugar, lard, coffee, and taters. While he was holding the gun on the company men, Dad said what time he was around organizing with the union there wasn't going to be no people going hungry . . . The men took the food out and distributed it according to the size of the families that was out on strike.

Sometimes after that he'd have to go off up there in the

mountains with the other miners. The thugs would try to catch them and make them come out. But he never would come out of the mountains when they come after him.

During all this time the thugs kept coming to our house a-searchin' for the machine gun that was used at Evarts. They'd come in and tear everything up, tear up the bed, cut open sacks of beans, a-lookin' for that machine gun.

One time when they come, Mommy told them they couldn't come in the house unless they left their guns outside. So they left their guns outside and come on in. They tore everything up. Mommy stood there and held a shotgun on them the whole time they was there. When they had finished searching for the machine gun, they started to leave. But Mommy held the shotgun on them and made them put everything right back just the way it had been before, made them clean up the house.

There was a lot of times Dad left the house and we didn't know where he went, what he was a-doin'. But sometimes he'd get up in the middle of the night and leave and we wouldn't see him for a week or maybe two weeks. Then he'd come back again, but he never could tell us where he'd gone. Most of the organizers had to keep their whereabouts kindly quiet.

I was younger then, about eight year old, and I didn't understand what was happening. So I asked Mommy what it was all about. She told me that what Daddy was doing wasn't wrong, that he was trying to take care of people that was hungry and starving, for little kids and for ourselves. And then I began to understand.

Dad knew who done the killings at Evarts, but he wouldn't tell. Course it was the gun thugs that started it.

The miners was just protecting theirselves. And the thugs never did find the machine gun.

Then they come to arrest Dad. They wanted to charge him with the killings at Evarts. But he wouldn't give hisself up. Our house set up on top of a hill and the gun thugs and John Henry Blair, the High Sheriff, started up the hill to the house. Dad made us get up under the house and barricade us in again, told Mom not to let us out for nothing. Then he laid down on the porch and aimed his shotgun at the thugs a-comin' up the hill. They told him, "We come to get you to take you to jail." He said, no, if they tried to take him off they'd have to meet this here lid (shotgun) he was holding on them. They never did come up the hill that time.

Well, it went on like that for a couple months. Then this one miner, he convinced Dad it would be better to give hisself up for the robbery, so he wouldn't get tried for murder. So in June he give hisself up. They come to the house after him and Dad made the thugs turn over their guns to him before he'd give hisself up. He told them, "If I give myself up, it's gonna be you walking in front of me all the way to the jailhouse, for I don't intend to take my last walk today." So Dad and Mommy held the guns on John Henry Blair and the thugs and marched them up the railroad tracks to the jailhouse. Then Dad give hisself up.

He stayed six months in Harlan County jail. When the trial come up they told him to leave Harlan County and never come back. He left Harlan and stayed gone about two years. Then he went back.

When Dad left Harlan, that's when we started a-hitchhikin'. When I was a kid I was on the road most of my life, Daddy moving us from one mining camp to another. I guess it might have had something to do with his organizing, him having to move around like that. But he always took Mom and us six kids with him.

We lived in Tennessee for a while and Dad worked in a wagon mine, where they use mules to haul the coal out. I used to go up there to the mine in the wintertime and haul four sacks of coal on my shoulder back to the house. I was about eleven then.

Me and my sisters worked with him at the mines. He never would let us go inside, but we did all the hauling on the outside.

Then we left Tennessee and he put us on the road again. We hitchhiked, all of us together, from Cane Creek, Tennessee, to Harlan, Kentucky. Of a night we'd sleep just anywhere we could find a place to sleep, a empty house, a barn . . . One night we was sleeping in a barn and I woke up and a big snake was lying beside me.

Then Dad got hurt in a slate fall in the mines in Cardinal, Kentucky. It broke his back. So me and Mom had to raise the family there for a while. This was in the summertime. She'd go out and pick huckleberries and blackberries and sell them that day for our food, for what we needed to eat and wear. Then the next day she'd go out again and pick more huckleberries and blackberries. Then she and I would go out in the cornfields and hoe corn for people. And we'd take in wash for people. Anything to bring in a little food.

When Dad got out of the hospital and back able to work again, he got us back on the road. We never settled in one place. This time we come back down towards Packard, Kentucky.

All of this time I was going to school about three months out of the year. Went as far as the fourth grade. It got to where I was ashamed of myself, I guess, so I got disinterested in it. I was kind of ashamed because everybody younger than me was in higher grades and it made me feel bad.

Finally, Mommy put her foot down and told Dad that we'd have to stay in one place long enough for us kids to go to school. So we stayed in Cardinal, Kentucky, up till I found somebody and married. Then I settled in Molus, Kentucky.

I married a coal miner. Before I ever married him I was staying at his place taking care of his wife. She was dying of cancer. I was fourteen then. We sat up day and night with her. I stayed there four years. She died the twentieth of March, 1940.

He didn't want me to leave him, but I went on home to Mom. Well, he was always good to me; I had always thought of him as a father. He was thirty years older than me. But I guess he was lonesome. So we ended up getting married and our first kid was born in '43.

In '44 my second boy was born. We called a doctor but we couldn't get him to come to the house. Rex was a hour and fifteen minutes old when the doctor got there and the doctor was drunk. I had four more kids after that.

Lonzo, my man, worked day and night in the mines. He'd come in of a night at four o'clock for his supper and then go right back in the mines again.

Whenever Lonzo would leave for the mines I was always scared I'd never see him again, that he'd be killed down in there. One time Lonzo got hurt real bad in the mines. Forty cars of coal rolled over his chest and caved it in. It broke his legs, broke his back, and caved his chest in. But he never did get no compensation for it.

Then when he died, I never did get no compensation. All the records about his accident had been kept in the union hall in Molus. But the union hall was burned to the ground and everybody's records were destroyed. So the union told me I didn't have no evidence that Lonzo had been hurt in the mines.

In February of '60, Mom told me the best thing I could do was to go up to Cincinnati and get me a job so I could support me and my kids. So I left the kids with her and came up here hunting me a job. There weren't no jobs for women in Kentucky.

I come up here and found me a job in a restaurant here in Over the Rhine. As soon as I got the job I went back for my kids and brought them up here with me.

I worked in the restaurant for a long time. The man who owned it and his wife were hillbillies too, so I didn't have too much trouble there. I was making a dollar an hour. Some days I'd get good tips and other days I didn't do so good.

While I was working in the restaurant, about all the people that come in there was from Kentucky, cause we served country food. One time a buckeye* come in there and started making fun of the way I talked. So I just hit him with a spatula. He never did bother me no more. He liked me after that.

---

* A native of Ohio.

Another time, there was this guy come in there and he was drunk. He ordered ham and eggs. He ate about half the eggs and then he just laid his face right down in the plate, right in the eggs. I went over to him and I said, "You better get your face up out of those eggs." Well, he raised up and looked at me, then he reached over and pinched me. So I hit him over the head with a ketchup bottle. I never did have too much trouble when I worked in the restaurant.

But that place is shut down now. That's what we need here again, is a hillbilly restaurant. If I could get the backing, I'd put me up a little place and call it the Hillbilly Country Kitchen.

There was a lot of Colored people that would come in the restaurant and get food. Most of the time they'd carry it out to eat it. They didn't have to do that, though. There's this one Colored guy, he asked me the other day when we was going to open up another hillbilly restaurant. Said he sure liked that good hillbilly food.

It was sort of hard when I first moved here because people was all the time calling me a hillbilly or throwing off on the way I talked. Buckeyes give hillbillies a bad time. They say these "dumb hillbillies don't know what they're doing." I'd always tell them I was proud to be a hillbilly. There was one man who would always throw off on the kind of food I eat. He said cornbread was for horses to eat.

The first building I ever lived in with my kids here had a lot of rats. The rats would get right up in the bed with the kids. The family that lived beneath us, a rat bit their baby.

After living in the country, living in an apartment house seemed like living in a jail till I got used to it. Even now I get restless, get out and take walks whenever I can, just to get outside.

Now, in the summertime, I'll just get out and walk and walk. I've been accused of a lot of things I didn't do just because I'm out walking. But I need to get out once in a while. I live here by myself now and it gets awful lonesome.

I guess that's why the kids here are always out in the streets. They feel penned up like they're in a jail in these small apartments. So they get out and walk the streets.

When I first moved here there was a gang of White kids used to come around here and throw rocks, break windows, swing from the fire escapes, and bust bottles down there in the alley. They quit as soon as it starts to get cold. Then the summertime comes and it starts right up again. But what else have they got to do around here?

Last summer, somebody give some money to the Appalachian Identity Center and Bill took the kids from the neighborhood on a field trip. They was gone a few days and the whole time they was gone things were real quiet around here. The kids need something to do. And Bill's got more than his hands full a-tryin' to keep that center going and a-workin' with the kids.

There's a lot of Colored people that lives here in Over the Rhine along with us hillbillies. And the Whites and Colored don't always get along too well with each other. But I've always got along good with Colored people.

Now, this alley right behind my apartment, that's where most of the time the Colored gangs and the White gangs meet to fight it out. They ain't got nothing else to do. They get restless and just take it out on each other.

It may seem dangerous for some women to walk the streets around here at night, but it don't seem that way to me. I've walked to work many of a night and never had much problem. A couple times some men have tried to follow me but I just break out in a run and leave them way behind.

I work in a vending machine factory now. Been there six years this April. We build the vending machines you see all over that says "Tom's" on them. I put panels in cabinets, put the shelves in, and pack and fill orders. I work on the line when I build cabinets. Then some days I build coin plates, where you put the coins in. It's interesting work. I like it. And most of the people that works there are hillbillies, all except one man. He's a buckeye but he acts just like a hillbilly.

If I ever retire, I might think about going back to Kentucky. But then I'd get down there and the winter would get rough and I'd get out of the notion of staying there. Really, though, I would live in Kentucky if they just had some factories for people to work in. And since the coal mining business has gone down, it seems like it just ain't like it used to be in the mountains. Things have changed a lot back in the mountains.

NO WOMAN CAN STAND ON A STREET CORNER
AROUND THIS NEIGHBORHOOD
Marie Wilson Chandler

I was born in Harlan County, Kentucky, in 1949, in a little coal mining town named Molus. I was born at home with one of these midwives. Her name was Linda Stevens. She wanted Mom and Dad to name me after her but Dad wanted me to be named Edith. And the midwife thought I should be named Linda cause she delivered me. So they ended up naming me Marie. But I never did find out if my name's Edith Marie or just Marie, because I never did have a birth certificate.

I was sick most of my life. I was real thin and had asthma a lot. In the house where we lived in Molus, we didn't have many beds and I slept on an old car seat right next to Mama and Daddy's bed. At night Mama and Daddy would rub my back to help me get to sleep.

When I was little, I would play with just about anything I could get my hands on. I used to shovel up dirt and make mud balls and then eat them by the spoonfuls. People say that dirt will hurt you and I tell them if it did I'd've been dead a long time ago.

Daddy, he drank a little, but he never did do nobody no harm. He'd come in when he'd been drinking and he'd get us up on his knee and start singing "John Henry." Sometimes I can sit and I can still hear my daddy singing "John Henry." I used to love to hear him sing that. He could really give a go at it. Daddy died when I was ten.

Sometimes Daddy would bring some friends to the

house to visit. I remember this one man come to the house, I guess I was about five or so. The man had shoes with laces on them. I asked the man how he got his shoes off when he went to bed at night. See, his shoes had laces on them and I had never had shoes with laces. I always had to wear combat boots with buckles, boots people had donated to me to wear. I never had a pair of shoes that tied. That's most of what I remember about when I was in the mountains.

I was eleven when Mom brought us up here. It was the first time I had ever seen a big city. I didn't know what to think about it. Mom put me in Washington Park School over here. Then I got sick and it turned out to be polio and spinal meningitis. I stayed in the hospital almost a year. They operated on my head right behind my left ear and then after a while I got better. I could walk again, but I had to learn all over how to walk and run.

When we moved up here, the building we lived in was a rat hole. The landlord never did like none of us kids. One day he come up to the apartment and said something or another mean to us, and my baby sister, Alice, she was just a little baby then, she cussed that man blue.

My sister and I slept in the same bed. Mom and five of us kids was living in this three-room place and we only had two beds. One night my sister woke me up. I was getting ready to roll over on a rat that had climbed in the bed with us. She pulled me over to her side of the bed and then she got the rat out. Lots of times I'd see them running across the room. My brothers would shoot them. That was down on Fourteenth Street.

In school over there at Washington Park, if you was

from Kentucky they would make fun of you. The kids would sit behind you in class and they'd snigger and make fun of you. It really hurt my feelings when they'd pop off at you cause you were a hillbilly. They used to say hillbillies had cooties. Like lice or something. I'd start crying, it hurt so bad. But after a while when they would throw sneers my way I didn't pay no attention to them. I wasn't going to let them hurt me no more.

Even now some words I say, they don't come out right, and people still laugh at me for the way I talk. Now I just tell them I talk the way I want to, the way I learned to talk, and nobody's going to change it. I like how I talk.

The teachers always told me not to use the word "ain't." They said there's no such word as "ain't." I says there are such a word as "ain't." I says, there's piss ain't and there's your ain't. So they didn't bother me too much then.

Then we moved from Fourteenth Street to Thirteenth Street. That's where I met Bill. I was in the sixth grade then. The building where he lived was right next to ours. I could step out of my window and go over on the fire escape where he lived.

Bill and I went together for about a year and then we broke up. He was dating this other girl and he used to come over to my place all the time and tell me all about her and the things they did together, like going to parties and everything. He also told me if I ever saw him on the street not to speak to him because somebody might see us and tell his girl friend. So then I quit talking to him on the street and he started getting mad about that.

I guess I started getting jealous. I didn't know if I was

falling in love with him or not. Pretty soon he'd come up to me on the street and start talking to me.

Bill was the first boy I went with in my whole life. I never went with another boy. While we was broke up, there was this boy that worked at the show house and he kind of liked me, but I didn't like him. One day I was sitting at the show house a-talkin' with him. I had my hair up in a bun. All of a sudden I felt somebody behind me pulling all the pins out of my hair and my hair falling down to my shoulders. Well, I turned around and it was Bill. We got back together after that and went together three years before we got married.

We got married July the twenty-fourth, 1966. Five days later Bill was sent to Vietnam. I stayed with his mom and on the weekends I'd go over and stay with my mom.

Bill come home in '67 and we had our first baby in '68. We have three little girls now and I never did have any trouble giving birth to any of them.

I'd like to have more kids, but not right now. Right now we just don't have the money, but someday I'd like to have more.

I enjoy staying at home and taking care of my kids. But I think every mother should get out away from their kids once in a while and go someplace, even for a couple of hours. But I think it's my place to take care of the kids. Bill, he works and brings in the money and it's my place to take care of the kids.

If I was to go out and get me a job, it would cost me more to pay a babysitter than what I would make on the job.

I just went through the ninth grade in school, but I

hope my girls will go on through college. That is, if I have the money to send them. And I would never force them to go if they didn't want to. Course I hated school.

Most of the time Bill and I try to make decisions about the family together. And like when Bill gets a paycheck, we pay the bills and if there's any left over we divide it between us. You very seldom see men that will do that for their wives.

If we've got any money left over, I take my share and go to Bingo once a week. I've kindly got hooked on Bingo, just like some people get hooked on drugs. One time I won a hundred dollars playing Bingo. I'm going again tomorrow night. Well, I don't have nothing else to do, except sit at home, take care of the kids. Sometimes I go down to the Center and stay with Bill and help him around there.

I try to get out of the house a lot. But it's kindly dangerous walking on these streets. No woman can stand on a corner around this neighborhood. Somebody always thinks you're a-hustlin'. Even when you walk from the house to the store there's always somebody tries to pick you up.

Sometimes I think about when I lived in Kentucky and I think about them as the good old days. Up here there's so much fighting and killing. You're scared to stick your head out the window, scared you might get it shot off, get it knocked off with a rock or something. Now, this Center here is the only place kids have to go to stay out of trouble.

In the summertime, when it gets hot, you'll never find me at home. I get out with the kids every chance I get. We usually wait till the sun goes down and it's not too hot and then we go down on the sidewalk and set on the curb with all the neighbors, and we all just set out there and talk. There's not really much else to do.

I REALLY KNOW WHAT IT MEANS
TO DO MAN'S WORK
Artie Chandler

I was born and raised in Whitley County, Kentucky, in a coal mining camp. My dad was a coal miner and there was eight of us children. We was all very happy. I went as far as the seventh grade in school.

When I growed up I married a coal miner. We lived in the coal fields around twenty-seven years and all that time he worked in the mines.

Every time George went off to the mines I was always worried about him, didn't know if I'd ever see him again. But that was our living and it was the only way we had to survive. When the mines run out there, we was forced to leave, to go somewhere and find work.

So about 1952, George went to Dayton, Ohio, and got him a job. We stayed there two years and then his job run out. Then we moved here to Cincinnati and we both went to work.

When we got here, one of the first jobs I got was in a factory and I was bringing home thirty-seven dollars a week. George wasn't working then. Sometimes the miner's asthma gets him to where he can't do nothing at all. I was paying fifteen dollars a week for rent. I went down to the welfare and asked them for some help. They just laughed in my face. They said I was making too much money to get on welfare. They don't like hillbillies down there at the welfare.

So then I worked in another factory that makes chairs. I was working on the assembly line. I found out real fast if you were a hillbilly people treated you pretty bad. And then I went to work in a factory that makes dinette furniture. I was the first woman in that factory to ever use a screwdriver.

I've worked all my life, I've done men's jobs, I've done everything. I've used screwdrivers, electric drills, punch presses. I really know what it means to do man's work. What gets me is you work all your life like a dog, you pay into these government programs. But still, when you need help, the people that's paid to help you they act like it's coming out of their own pocket.

George had a stroke not long ago. We were living with Bill and Marie then, all of us together, just trying to make it on what money we could bring in. I've always worked all my life and I never had to do this before, but when George had the stroke I knew I needed some help. I had to quit my job to take care of him and there was no way Bill could support the seven of us even on the two jobs he works.

So I went down to the welfare and told them I needed help. They said as long as we were living with Bill it was his responsibility to take care of us. If we wanted help, we'd have to move out. The trouble was we didn't have any money to rent a place.

Finally they gave me ten dollars and a quarter for a month's rent and eighteen dollars and a nickel for a month's food. I had to take it cause we didn't have anything at all and George was in the hospital.

When I knew I needed some help, I went up here to this place called Hub Center where they're supposed to help people. Well, I told this young kid that was working there that we was starving and didn't have the money to pay our rent or buy our medicine. Well, he started writing something down on a slip of paper, and he wrote for the longest time. Then he give it to me and he said, "Take this here paper to 1631 Vine Street and they'll give you a sandwich." I said, "Thanks for nothing, kid." I never was so embarrassed in all my life. I thought, well, I know I have to be going crazy. I just have to be, this just can't be happening.

So one day on a Sunday I got real sick late in the night and Bill carried me to the doctor. By this time the welfare had sent me to the public clinic and they had given me a lot of pills that made me real sick. So I went to this doctor and he asked me if I had ever considered going to see a psychiatrist. I said, no, I hadn't, but I'll go just to see if I really am going crazy.

I told the psychiatrist all my troubles. I told him I thought I might be going crazy. He just laughed at that and said I had a serious nerve problem. Then he called the welfare department and told them to quit making me take all these pills they had give me. He told me to stay on these here nerve pills—librium—and see if they wouldn't help me. But they make me sick too.

Not long after that I got a letter from the welfare telling me if I didn't go down to the Red Cross and sign up for work, they'd close our case.

Finally we got a check for eighty dollars from the welfare. I thought that was for groceries and that they'd also pay our rent money. We had had to move out of Bill's to get any help. So I went out and bought some groceries with the money. Then I found out the welfare expected us to live—food, rent, and all—on eighty dollars a month. The rent here is seventy-six dollars on this place. That would give us four dollars a month for food.

So when I realized what I had done, I called this Colored man that rents these apartments. He said to me that the welfare was doing me wrong and he would help me. So he called the welfare and told them they were supposed to be paying me a hundred and thirty-one dollars a month and they'd better give me the rest cause he was sending me down there after it. I found out from that Colored man that there are a few nice people.

I went down to the welfare and they wouldn't let me talk to the caseworker. But I sat in that office for two hours and didn't move until they brought me out that voucher for my rent. Then I took it over to the landlord and paid him. I still don't know if I'm on welfare or not, or if they'll ever send me another check.

I've called over there so many times asking for my caseworker and they always say he's out of the office, or away from his desk, or he's not available to come to the phone. And I've gone over there and tried to see him, but they'll never let me see him.

So one day I called this woman that works there and told her I wanted to talk to my caseworker. And she said, well, didn't I know he was a very busy man, she said, "Don't you realize nothing?" And then the hillbilly come out in me. I said, "I know enough that if a man works there he's got to be at his desk once in a while." I said, "Let me tell you something. I'm getting wore out. You take the welfare, the building, and all and stick it, because I'll never beg you for another dime."

Whenever you try to get help around here, all you have to do is tell them you're from Kentucky and that's it. They act like you're so stupid you don't know what you're doing. Whenever the buckeyes get mad at you the first thing they can think of is to say, "You're just an of hillbilly; you ain't nothin' but a briarhopper, you just look like one." I just say, well, that makes me happy. But sometimes I really cut loose and get nasty when they call me names.

I just hope something will come up that we can get completely off this welfare. Maybe someday George's black lung disability will come through.

All our lives George and I have shared everything. We both worked and helped each other with the groceries and the bills and everything. We did everything together. Now that he's sick I've found out what it is to have to do it all on your own.

I never go out of the house any more. I can't leave George here alone cause I'm afraid he's going to fall or hurt hisself some way. So I stay in the house all the time.

All we can do now is hope. Maybe there's some way we can find to make it, to survive. If we find a way, I imagine we'll go back home to Kentucky and just stay there till we die.

About eleven o'clock at night, I finished my last conversations with the Wilsons and Chandlers, the conversations that would be used to create their chapters of this book. Marie and Bill and I left the Appalachian Identity Center, picked up their children at Artie's house, and went back to their apartment on Thirteenth Street.

Outside, all along Vine Street, neon lights were blazing everywhere, music was blaring loud and raucously from somewhere up the street, cars were still moving up and down the streets in Over the Rhine. Two girls were standing on the corner of Thirteenth and Vine, young and heavily painted and hoping to make a few dollars that night. An old man in ragged work clothes tottered drunkenly down Vine and turned into an alley.

The streets and alleys were littered with empty whiskey bottles, discarded papers and garbage. A huge rat jumped out of a pile of garbage and scurried across the street. Broken glass was everywhere. It was a normal night in Over the Rhine.

We walked up the flight of stairs to Marie and Bill's apartment. Marie and Bill went into the bedroom and put the two younger girls to bed. The oldest girl came into the front room and sat down beside me. She was eating a tangerine and talking to me about her nursery school. Every once in a while she would look rather suspiciously at my banjo laying next to me on the couch. Finally she asked me to play her a tune.

We picked and sang together for a while and as I watched her simultaneously munching tangerine sections and singing, I felt a wave of deep emotion go through me. It hit me then

1. FLORENCE REECE

2. GRANNY HAGER

3. GRANNY HAGER

4. BETTY MESSER SMITH AND DAISY MESSER (L. TO R.)

5. KATHERINE TILLER

6. SHIRLEY DALTON

7. DELLA MAE SMITH

8. WYOMING WILSON

9. MARIE CHANDLER

10. ARTIE CHANDLER

11. MYRA WATSON

12. MYRA WATSON

13. EFFIE WOODIE

14. EFFIE WOODIE

15. ELLEN RECTOR

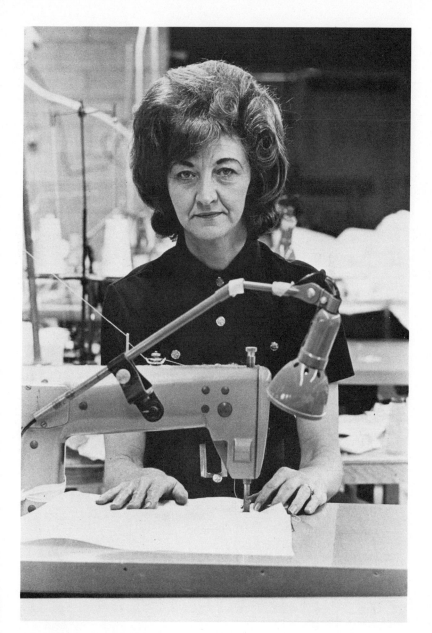

16. BERNICE RATCLIFF

17. LORINE MILLER

SUMMEROUR

DAVID A.
BORN
MAR. 23, 1889
FEB. 12, 1968

ELIZABETH
WIFE BORN
JAN. 1 8
FEB.

18. SHIRLEY SUMMEROUR

19. DONNA REDMUND

20. RUBY GREEN

21. NANCY KINCAID

that this little girl, born and raised in Over the Rhine, still had the inherited love of old-time country music. She was a hillbilly and would grow up being proud of it. Then she ate another tangerine and conked out for the night. I thought of my two hillbilly babies back home in the mountains and hoped that they too slept well that night.

Marie and Bill and I stayed up until after four in the morning. We sat around their kitchen table and talked a lot about our lives, shared a few good laughs and a great meal cooked by Bill, who seems to be an expert chef. We talked mostly about what was happening to hillbillies in Over the Rhine. Bill and Marie don't seem to expect any great changes in the conditions of the slum in the near future. They are the kind of people who take it a day at a time and do what they can to help their neighbors and kin because they really care about people. But having spent most of their lives in the slum, they are realistic in their approach to the problems of the people there. If there ever are any changes for the better in Over the Rhine, they will come about through the efforts of Bill and Marie and people like them.

When it was time to turn in, they gave me a good bed in a warm room. I had three hours to sleep before I had to leave the city. And while I slept I dreamed.

I dreamed of Tom Hicks robbing the company store, of Wyoming hitting the guy with the spatula. And I saw Artie as she looked the first time I met her, a long time before George had his stroke and she a nervous breakdown. I saw Marie sitting on the curb talking with her neighbors.

Marie woke me at seven o'clock; she had already made the coffee she knew I would need. And when I finally left them, I wanted to say a lot of things to them. But the words wouldn't come out. I felt the kind of sorrow and pain you feel when you're leaving good friends, not knowing what will happen to them.

Over the Rhine is probably one of the ugliest slums I have ever seen. It has nothing of material value to offer people who might visit there. But in that dirty, rat-infested slum I felt the warmth, the strength, the courage and gentleness of the Blue Ridge Mountain refugees who fight and love their way through the city jungle searching for hillbilly heaven.

Part Three

MILL MOTHER'S LAMENT

MILL MOTHER'S LAMENT
BY ELLA MAE WIGGINS

We leave our homes in the morning,
We kiss our children good-bye,
While we slave for the bosses,
Our children scream and cry.

And when we draw our money,
Our grocery bills to pay,
Not a cent to spend for clothing,
Not a cent to lay away.

And on that very evening,
Our little son will say:
"I need some shoes, Mother,
And so does sister May."

How it grieves the heart of a mother,
You every one must know,
But we can't buy for our children,
Our wages are too low.

It is for our little children,
That seem to us so dear,
But for us nor them, dear workers,
The bosses do not care.

But understand, all workers,
Our union they do fear;
Let's stand together, workers,
And have a union here.

You Never Lose Nothing
by Being Good to Folks

MYRA WATSON

PRATHERS CREEK, NORTH CAROLINA

My memories of that mountain farm
Are driven like snow before the storm,
And the faces of my friends and kin
Are scattered just like straw in the wind.

When the Appalachian Mountains reach into North Carolina they start to roll. From the Virginia border, right at Galax, the mountains take on a greener hue and show the signs of well-kept farmland. Rocks jut out everywhere in the green pastureland, but the Guernsey cows feed around them from the rich fescue grass.

Prathers Creek community is right at the tip of the North Carolina border. Route 221 runs west from Sparta, the county seat, right through the center of the community on its way to the tourist town of Boone. The road has been paved only a few years now, and when the pavement went through it took part of Myra Watson's front yard. Likewise, when Route 113 was paved north to the Virginia line it cut right past the front door of Effie Woodie's house. Surrounding the two highways there is rich farmland, good for raising burley tobacco and dairy and beef cattle.

There are few jobs available other than farming for the residents of Prathers Creek. Some of the younger generation work in the garment factories in Sparta, North Carolina, and Independence, Virginia. A few people, like Effie's husband, Eef, draw disability checks because of injuries suffered when they were children or because of accidents in the garment factories. One man draws a disability check because of injuries he got in the Kentucky coal mines where he migrated to find work in the twenties.

Prathers Creek didn't roar in the twenties. There were a few roadsters running along the dirt roads and every Saturday night somebody had a "play party," as mountain dances were often called since the local churches looked down on dancing. But mostly Prathers Creek was a tranquil farming community where farmers raised tobacco and where the biggest social gathering came in the fall of the year when it came time to grade the tobacco. Then, as now, neighbors and kin would gather in the barns on the little farms and exchange ghost stories while they divided the burley tobacco leaves into three different grades of quality and size: tips, brights, and lugs.

When the Depression hit Prathers Creek in the thirties times were even harder for the farmers. Some of the men, including Myra Watson's husband, got jobs on the Works Progress Administration (WPA) while Myra and other women worked out in the fields for fifty cents a week. Homemade whiskey was about the only thing that sold well and most everybody drowned their own depression in a little white liquor now and then. Hoover's Panic was real to the people of Prathers Creek. Food was scarce and clothes were sewn by hand in the lamp-light.

There used to be a post office in Prathers Creek. Effie Woodie opened one in the forties. Everybody went to Effie's post office to get their mail, buy a plug of chewing tobacco or a sack of corn meal, and to pass the time of day.

Most of the old homeplaces in Prathers Creek are still oc-cupied, if not by people, by bales of hay and an occasional nanny goat. Most all the houses in the community were built in the early twenties; large two-story frame buildings with a lot of gingerbread and porch posts. But the more modest homeplaces of an earlier day still stand too, like Myra Watson's homeplace over near Antioch church. It is a rough-hewn frame, one story and three rooms. Unpainted and sturdy, it stands beside an old apple tree down in a hollow, promising to stand for many years to come.

On Saturday nights Prathers Creek comes alive. Drive-in movies have substituted for play parties, fast hot rods make the trip to the Sparta Drive-in swift though dangerous over the mountain roads. And, while the young court the pleasures of romance and adventure and bonded whiskey, the older folks sit around home and play a little old-time music and drink the real stuff.

Prathers Creek is losing its population faster than it is gain-ing. It is no longer financially possible to make a good living off the land. The small farms provide barely a subsistence liv-ing for the older folks, who just get by on an income from their burley tobacco sales and small Social Security checks.

The younger generation is almost gone now, having been forced to migrate to places like Winston-Salem, North Carolina, to find jobs in the garment factories and cotton mills. Isolated far back in the mountains away from industry and progress, the little community is inhabited mostly by older folks now.

The creeks that flow beside the mountain farms still run clean and fresh. The mountains, though stripped of much timber, are still covered with wildflowers and ginseng. The loudest noise you can hear at night is the sound of the crickets singing their same old-timey tune. Perhaps that is the most disturbing thing about Prathers Creek today. It is so quiet.

I can remember my great-grandfather, that's as far back as I can remember on the Estep side. But I can't remember none on my Irvin side, no farther than my grandmother Irwin. They all died before I was old enough, and some of them before I was even born. Barry Estep, he married Lou Owsley, in Wilkes County, before moving to Alleghany County. And Grampa Barry's brother William, he moved to Virginia. Their first child, John Wesley, was born August 8, 1848. This was my great-great-grandfather.

My grandaddy was a Confederate soldier. He lived to be ninety-six years old. And he fought in the Confederate War. Went in, they drafted him when he was sixteen years old. He didn't tell me too much about it. But my grandmother, she said that the deserters, that wouldn't go, they'd come to the house and they'd steal everything they had. They had Home Guards to guard the people, but they couldn't guard them all, you know. They'd come and steal your milk and steal your corn and steal your flour away from the women and children that the husbands was serving in that war.

This land was all cleared when I grew up. But you know, my grandaddy, when he bought that land over yonder, I think he said he swapped a horse, give a horse, and so many bushel of corn, for a farm. But it was yet all in woods, you know, he had to clear it up and work on it.

When I was a child—see, I'm sixty-five years old— when I was going to school, I had two school dresses. Well, I put on a clean one on Monday morning, and I had to wear that dress till Friday. Then I got a clean dress on Friday. I had one pair of Sunday shoes. Now I wore these old brogans and old yarn knit socks to school. And as I grew on up it was the same thing until after I got up about fifteen or sixteen years old.

We never went to the store and bought a thing in the world except some coffee and sugar. Now that's what's bought out of the store. We raised the rest of it. Everybody raised stuff at that time. And just as long as the Lord blessed you to make a garden, and potatoes, and corn, that's what we lived on. We raised our hogs, we raised our corn to make our hogs, and we raised our corn to feed our cows. We never got no corn liquor out of our corn, no, not a bit. We butchered our own hogs, and made our own flour, took it to our own mill and ground it, and milked our own cows and made our own butter.

Why, there wasn't no such thing to buy then, as cow's milk butter, unless they might've took it in to the store.

Now, when you make butter, you skim the cream off the milk, and you sit that up and let it sour. And then you can churn it up and down, with an old-timey churner, or you can shake it in a can. Well, then, the butter'll come, and it'll separate from the milk. Then you dip your butter out, and wash it, wash all the milk out, and then you put a little salt in it, and cut it up, come to the table and eat it.

And then, after I got up big enough to go anywhere, you couldn't go, you had no automobile. You walked, or went in steer wagons, or we went in a horse and buggy, or just any way we could get there. But there sure wasn't an automobile to take you in.

Hoover's Panic, that brought us down still lower, when that come. You couldn't buy nothing, you couldn't get a job. My husband walked, I'd say eight miles, and worked all day for eighty cents. You had to have food stamps to get what you got with. There was no automobile running then. Course we had one, but we sure couldn't afford to drive it. And then after Roosevelt got in, things begin to pick up a little. He passed the Social Security, and he fixed up the WPA for men to get a job, to build these roads and things like that. We didn't have nothing but mud roads. And he got them graveled, that took a change.

Now let me tell you, Hoover days was tough. Everybody was making whiskey that could get a place to stick a still. We couldn't even get enough money together to buy us a pound of coffee. And John Reeves, my husband, just had one pair of overalls, good overalls, to his back. I don't know whether I had ary a dress or not. But his grandmother and his sister was there with us at that time, they was staying there. But she'd get out and help Uncle Mann Williams hoe corn, and bring in a dollar or two, once in a while. She got a dollar a week for staying with people. One dollar a week. There wasn't nothing you could do, unless you went out and helped somebody hoe corn or stayed with somebody, helped out in sickness.

Now, I tell you when the first time I ever had electricity was, in nineteen and forty-four, when my daddy died, and I moved here. That was the first electricity I ever had. We used kerosene lamps. Used lamps and lanterns, just lamps and lanterns. And we cooked on a wood stove. Way back yonder when I was just a kid a-growin' up, you know, my grandmother she cooked everything on the fireplace, in old black pots. And everything she cooked was cooked in those pots. And we'd bake bread in the skillet. We'd dip down the coals and put on the hearth, and then we'd put the skillet on there and let it get hot, and then we'd put a lid on the fire, let it get hot. Then we'd put our bread in the skillet, and we'd set our lid on it and put coals on top of the skillet lid.

My mother died at the age of eighty-four, and she wouldn't have a biscuit baked in that electric stove. I had to put a fire in that wood stove every morning to bake biscuits.

Last year was the first time I ever had oil heat or a bathroom. Let's see now . . . I was sixty-four when we got in the bathroom. I was sixty-four years old before I ever had a bathroom, hot or cold water. I'd run out doors, I'd go behind the house. And I was past sixty-five before I ever had oil heat. Young'uns, it's costed awful, but I've kept babies to pay for it, and I'm glad I've had it.

Everybody in Prathers Creek came to see Aunt Myra Watson's new bathroom. What was curious about the bathroom was not its shiny new fixtures. Many families in the community already had indoor plumbing. What *was* curious about the bathroom was that after sixty-odd years Myra Watson had finally been able to afford it.

Myra has always been poor in money. The fruits of her labor have been consumed by hungry orphan children and bedridden old people. When she is not tending her garden or milking the cows or birthing a calf, Auntie is laboring over the sick, the very small, and the forgotten people.

She waits on them, feeds and clothes them. She administers her time-proven remedies to make them well. When my oldest baby was sick with a fever, Auntie used to rub polecat grease, the grease rendered from a skunk, all over his chest and limbs. Within a few hours, by the time the smell had worn off, the fever had subsided. And always, without fail, that polecat grease has brought her tiny patients' fevers back down to normal.

Auntie has a remedy for every illness. One winter while I was living with Auntie I had the flu and was burning up with a fever. Auntie got hold of some white liquor and set it in a frying pan. She struck a match and held it to the whiskey. Then she fed it to me by the spoonfuls. And I didn't fight that fever, I just laughed it down. With Auntie's remedies, adults are luckier than children.

I don't know, I'm a funny person, but I'm a great believer in what you do for people, can help them out in any way or how, I feel like you'll be rewarded. It's just the way I feel, and just the way I've always been. And there hain't nobody that stands on the face of this green earth that could ask me to help them or accommodate them, and if I could, I would. Black nor White. Now that's just my nature.

I went to church one day, and I just had one dollar. Well, I give it to the preacher. And I come on back, I said, "Jean, I give the preacher the last dollar we had." She says, "Law me, Momma, what'll we do now?" I says, "Well, it'll be returned threefold." So the next day in the mail I got two dollars in money from my cousin up in Maryland. So I said, "Now, Jean, you see."

They was a family when we lived over here at the old place, and they had a whole house full of young'uns. Well, their mother got sick, and then she had her little baby. And there was nobody on earth to turn a tap of nothing, only just them little bitty young'uns. So, I leaves my home every day, and I goes up there every day and dresses that baby, and tend to that woman, and cook food and take it to them. And I was awful glad of that. I had a good clear and acquitted conscience. That was Jess Wilder's family.

And I've picked up more little tired young'uns around, that didn't have no home. Now there was Jean, I took her when she was three weeks old. She was a 'gitimate—or whatever you call it—child. And her mother didn't have no mind, you see? She was out on the mercy of the people. Well, they let me keep her till she was nine months old. And they was going to put her out for adoption. Well, then, when she was four years old they brought

123

her back. And they couldn't get nobody on earth no-where to keep her. John Reeves, my husband, he says to me, "Now, you can't keep her." I says, "The Bible says, 'Turn no one away from your door, for you know not who it may be.'" I says, "I'm keeping her." I was right here in the bed, sick, couldn't even raise my head off the pillow. "Well, all right." Jean, I've had her ever since. And when I was left by *my* self, look what a blessing she's proved to me.

I raised six children. And one of them was a Black 'un. He was about eleven years old, but he was very small for his age. And that boy was just as good to me as he could be. John Reeves was hauling coal all the time, and he'd get with him and want to go with him after the coal.

Well, the little feller's mother and dad was both dead. And he had nowhere to go, nowhere to stay, and he had on a pair of shoes that was too big, his feet was just rubbed raw. Well, John Reeves kept telling me, "I'm going to bring Buckwheat home one evening." They called him Buckwheat. And I said, "You know I don't like Colored people." Well, he brought that little nasty rascal up here, and I said the next morning, I said, "All right. That boy don't stay here. Unless you take him to town, buy him some shoes and some clothes," I says, "he ain't staying at my house." Well, John Reeves took him off and dressed him up, got him good clothes, and give him a bath and come back. And he stayed here till he was twenty-some years old. Till he went off with John Reeves up there to the sawmill.

And you know what? Young'uns, I'll tell you all right

now. I never lost nothing in my life by being good to people. People thinks you will, they think you can't do that. But you never lose a thing in the world by being good to folk.

The name "Myra" means "one who has shed many tears." It is a fitting name for Auntie. But she does not cry for herself. She cries because babies are hungry and there is no food. She cries because people are sick and they hurt and she can feel their pain. She cries, for the dying, tears of hope.

Auntie's hope for herself is in the next world. Her burial insurance is paid up and already a gravestone stands ready to be marked with her name in the New Hope cemetery at Antioch.

In Auntie's heaven there is no sickness, no hard labor, no suffering, and you don't need money to survive. And the only tears shed are tears of joy.

Lord, Have Mercy, Give Me That Gun!

EFFIE WOODIE
SOUR HILL, PRATHERS CREEK, NORTH CAROLINA

The tunes I danced to long ago
The squeak of the fiddle, the scrape of the bow,
The young men in their shoes so fine
That courted me in my younger time.

Effie Woodie is probably the most slender woman in the world. To look at her sideways is not to see her at all. But she can move like a cyclone, her willow frame stirring little air as she goes. She has the energy of a hound chasing a rabbit, the eyes of a girl well courted; her chestnut brown hair is only now beginning to show signs of turning gray.

If you ever go to visit Effie and her husband, Eef, you are likely to find her making "leather britches"—green beans strung up to dry for the winter—or churning butter or making cottage cheese. Effie keeps busy with her household chores and often minds her grandson, Tommy, while she works in the kitchen. And sometimes it is possible to get her to sit down for a few minutes over a cup of coffee and a Salem and listen to her talk about the old days.

I was the little squirt at home. My older brother, he quit school and went to West Virginia hunting him a job. My daddy was always a farmer, but in the hard times he worked on them roads, on the WPA, worked for anybody he could for just about any amount of money he could.

Then my grandmother died. It was during the Panic and we didn't have no money. So my daddy, he sold the cow to pay on her funeral bill. Then not long after that we found out my brother was dead. Well, Daddy went after him and he just had one greenback dollar. So he went on down to Sparta, to old man Rufe Doughton, and borrowed twenty-five dollars and buried my brother. That's been about forty years ago.

When I was a-growin' up I knowed Myra and we'd go out together and dig roots, just all kinds of roots. Mama'd help us to dry them. Then Papa'd go to Wilkesboro maybe once every week or two; he'd take the wagon. It'd take him three days and two nights to go there and get back. Well, he'd take the dried roots and buy bolts of cloth to make our clothes and to make the bedclothes.

I remember my daddy telling us when we got big enough to pick up a pebble we was big enough to help out on the farm. And I hated them pebbles; I hated to haul rock, and it seemed like he could find the most rocks of anybody I ever seen.

We dried apples in the fall of the year. We'd come in

from school. We had three miles to walk to school and back. Mama'd have big old tubs of apples already peeled by hand. Well, in the night we had to get up our school work, then we had to cut apples. Many of a night I went to sleep cutting apples. Next day Mama'd put them out in the sunshine to dry them. Then Papa'd haul them to Wilkesboro, what we didn't need to eat. And that bought more material, to make our little clothes for winter. Mama made our coats, knitted our little tams, our wool stockings, and made all of our dresses.

We couldn't buy just anything, only what we needed. Mama, she'd churn butter and we'd take it to the store to sell. We'd take big fat old hens to the store and we got the things we needed by trading the butter and hens.

We made our flour, raised wheat and rye. I worked in the wheat and the rye; helped stack it, haul it, and thresh it. Then after I'd finished I had to run to the house and help Mama on that old cook stove, cooking for all those men who worked at the sawmill and boarded with us. Then I'd go to bed, just about fall in.

We had the washing to do down at the spring. We carried it down there and did it out in big old pots, used homemade soap, on the washboard. The older ones would beat out their clothes with a paddle, but I was too little to do that.

I never had but one pair of shoes. My daddy would carry my shoes and my white stockings to church in his pocket, nearly to the churchhouse door, and I'd go barefooted. Mama carried an old wet rag to wipe my feet off just as soon as we got near the church. Then she'd put my white stockings and my shoes on. And we went on in. It was about two miles and a half from our house to the church and we walked through the mountains to get there.

I remember Mama fixing baskets of food for families that was starving and I was wondering what we'd have left to eat. But she'd send it on. She'd say, "They're hungry, you gotta go take them this food." She'd send my daddy. That was when that awful flu hit the country and everybody was dying of it. Daddy went day and night bringing them food. And he buried the dead by hisself. He'd have to go in and bathe them and dress them and put them in the casket. Other people's afraid to go in.

Mama didn't have a sewing machine. She would sit up of a night and sew with her fingers the clothes for all of us. I remember her sitting up all night making shrouds for dead people. My grandpa'd make the caskets and then line them with wool Mama had spun and then put material over that. Then Mama would do all the finger work by lamplight.

After the cotton mills opened up in Highpoint, Mama would get these old ruined pieces of yarn from the mills and crochet for people. She'd pick it all apart and put it on her spinning wheel and make a strong thread out of it. She'd double and twist it somehow.

When I entered high school I had three print dresses to wear to school. And then I had a little better one to wear on weekends. All we had was cotton dresses, all winter long. And we wore cotton hose. They'd come wholesale, they'd come with holes in them. But we'd patch them, we didn't care about wearing patches.

One day Papa got me some knee socks that was on sale. Oh, I was pleased to death. But Mama made me promise I wouldn't wear them without hose underneath. So I had to wear them with my hose.

The first payday I ever got, I was just out of high school. This man had a patch of beans, he called them "red valentines." He wanted me to pick the beans and he give me twelve and a half cents an hour. I could go from his field across the creek to the country store. There we could buy material to make dresses—eight cents a yard. We'd carry it back home and Mama'd make clothes for us. I was so proud to make twelve and a half cents an hour. And now my children would die if they had to come down to such as that.

I wanted to study nursing in school, but I got knocked out of that. So then I decided to take a business course. I borrowed the money and worked on the road to pay it back. I worked building side roads. I finished the business course in nine months. It was the Twentieth Century system that come up from Winston to Sparta.

After Effie finished business school she began looking for a job. But Hoover's Panic had hit the country hard and there were no jobs for her. She left the mountains and migrated to Highpoint in the North Carolina piedmont. But even in the city she couldn't find work, and the climate was uncomfortably hot for a mountain girl. So she returned to the mountains and went to work on her father's farm.

Although she had many suitors, Effie did not marry until she was twenty-seven years old. Then she married Ephraim Woodie. Eef and Effie's personalities are like their names—they match. Her talents are in butter churning, gardening, and working with people. Eef makes the meanest home brew in the Blue Ridge Mountains, picks and sings country style, and is known for his ability to hold a chaw of tobacco in his mouth for several hours without spitting.

Before they were married, Eef had a band called "Ephraim Woodie and the Henpecked Husbands," which traveled through the mountains in the twenties bringing old-time music to old-time folks. The string band recorded several 78 RPMs for RCA Victor which are still popular as far away as London, England.

When Effie and Eef married, Eef gave up his roaming but not his singing, and Effie began a long struggle to support herself, her disabled husband, and their three children. She applied for a job as postmistress for Prathers Creek community and got it.

This house we live in now up here on Sour Hill was the post office for Prathers Creek, the grocery store, and our home. And we had a gas pump I run out in front. I raised the children right here in this store while I was a-workin'.

See, when Eef was a baby, only three years old, he lived in that old log cabin with his daddy and mama. Well, one night his flannelette gown caught fire and he was burned so bad his eyes was ruined. The doctors claim that's what caused the cataracts on Eef's eyes.

Eef went to blind school and they taught him Braille until his eyes got right. Then they took them cataracts off. Of course it has disfigured his vision. But while he was totally blind they taught him how to cane chairs and make brooms. Now that he's old he can see just as good as I can, and every broom I get he examines them and tells me how cheap and how no count they are.

My two boys were born over there in that log cabin. When Russell was born I never did have but two big pains with him. And I laughed at everyone, them a-tellin' jokes. There was a woman there and the doctor told her to give me a little chloroform every time a pain hit me hard. I'd turn my head to keep from getting it. And I heard Russell cry when he was born.

Effie raised three children in her post office. She would set the children on the wooden floor to play while she waited on her customers. Whenever she had a free moment, Effie did her household chores. She did all her wash by hand.

Every day, no matter what the weather was like, Effie had to walk down the mountain carrying a satchel she called her "post office" to pick up the mail. Once, she was found lying at the foot of the mountain almost dead with frostbite.

Effie's father was a Democrat and that eventually meant trouble for a young woman who was not very political herself. In 1952, when the Eisenhower administration took over the country and its post offices, Effie lost her job to the Republicans. She closed her post office/grocery store and went to work in the fields picking strawberries and beans.

But Effie has led an interesting life up on Sour Hill. The neighbors have almost always been good to Effie and she remembers both the good and the bad times.

At that time all my neighbors was Black folks. They called the place where they lived Sweet Holler. Our little house set up on the peak of the hill so I just named it Sour Hill.

Seems like my neighbors was a lot better to me in a way than other folks. And they never did to me no damage. Except when Mut went crazy. And of course he couldn't help that. Mut took me to the hospital to have one of my children.

Well, Mut drank liquor and doped till it just burnt his brain. He come back one night a-wantin' my daughter Dolores. She was thirteen then. Wanted to take her to heaven. He thought he was God.

He come one night at midnight. He didn't have a gun on him, nor a knife, he didn't have nothing. Parked his car out in front of our house and at first he just hollered for Dolores. "C'mon, honey, I'm going to put you in heaven," he says. Says, "I got Eef and Effie in hell and now I'm going to put you in heaven."

Russell told Eef to get the shotgun and Russell got the rifle. Mut had started to bust the door down. They meant to cripple him, they didn't want to kill him. He had his face up against the door. I said, "Lord, have mercy, I can't stand no more! Give me that gun!" I grabbed the gun out of Russell's hands and I pointed it right at Mut's head. Russell jumped me and knocked the gun out of my hand. He knocked me to the floor and I grabbed the gun again, but he wrassled me around and got it away from me.

Well, the law finally come. We got them there in three hours and forty-five minutes. We had the light on him outside. He was standing there blowing the millers and moths around the light when the law come. They clipped a handcuff on him and tried to get him in the patrol car. When Russell went out on the porch to see if Mut had calmed down any, Mut lunged at him, just lunged away from them patrols. They had to put another hand-cuff on him.

They said it was so hard on him going down to Sparta with the patrols that he cut his wrists all to pieces. And I grieved and cried over that so. I couldn't help but feel sorry for him.

Effie has compassion for other people, but she has other emotions too. Whenever Effie feels that people are not being treated fairly, her anger takes hold of her. Such was the case with the Pine Ridge Craft Cooperative.

The history of the Pine Ridge Co-op is long and involved, but, basically, the craft cooperative was organized, owned, and operated by poor people in Alleghany County, North Carolina, and Effie Woodie and Myra Watson were among its members. Beginning in 1968, poor but extremely talented mountain people in Alleghany County started bringing in a little extra family income through the production of home-made crafts.

Members of Pine Ridge Co-op rented a shop building in Sparta, the county seat, and sold hand-carved wooden dolls, hand-sewn quilts, expertly crafted gun cabinets, and other traditional mountain crafts to tourists passing through the Blue Ridge Mountains. The cooperative operated on a shoe-string and received token organizational assistance from the local antipoverty agency. It was the opinion of some highly placed staff members in the antipoverty agency that this organization of poor people was not feasible. They failed to recognize, however, that the craft co-op was something the poor people wanted and had themselves organized.

Craftsmanship is a tradition in the Southern mountains and mountain people pride themselves on the fine homemade items they made first out of necessity for survival and later even for the enjoyment of more affluent people who usually pay ridiculously low prices for objects representing many hours of labor and incredible skill.

It should not be necessary for poor mountain people to have to eke out a small part of their living from the sales of some of America's finest craftsmanship. Mountain people have always been expert musical instrument builders, furniture makers, and seamstresses, and the members of the Pine Ridge Craft Co-op joined the ranks of thousands of other hillbillies who hoped to supplement a meager family income with the sales of their crafts. They were not getting rich but they were working together on tasks that they enjoyed.

While the Pine Ridge Co-op began its operation, the local antipoverty agency remained in the background watching. When business began to go well for the co-op and its membership of about forty families, the antipoverty agency stepped in and attempted to claim credit for its success. Which brings us back to Effie Woodie and her anger.

During a face-to-face confrontation with the poverty agency and its domineering director, the co-op members tried to speak but were silenced time and again. Finally, in a desperate move to be heard, Effie lunged at the agency's director and challenged her to a fist-and-claw fight hillbilly style. But there was no fight. Effie was held off by friends who knew that despite her opponent's considerable weight advantage, Effie would have won hands down, and no one had the money to bail her out of jail. One thing though is certain. Some antipoverty folks will think twice before they travel up on Sour Hill. Effie Woodie lives there and she wields a mean butter paddle.

What Ain't Called Melungeons
Is Called Hillbillies

ELLEN RECTOR
SNEEDVILLE, TENNESSEE

There ain't no tarpaper shacks in heaven,
The Lord will be my landlord there,
The creeks are bright and clear in heaven,
There ain't no coal dust in the air.

Old-time religion is good enough for Ellen Rector. A handsomely sturdy woman, Ellen obviously has found joy and comfort in her Primitive Baptist faith. Her eyes have a sparkle and her lips a smile which might well date back to that cold winter day when she was immersed in the icy waters of a mountain creek, the promise of her salvation spoken by a Hard-Shell Baptist preacher dressed in his Sunday best.

Religion is as much a part of hillbilly people's lives as music. Ellen combines both at revivals and church meetings, where she brings spiritual renewal to her brothers and sisters with her gospel songs. Her fine country voice has a resonance that rings through the wooden frame churches and the camp meeting tents. Her songs are prayers and stories at the same time—the stories of life's daily toil and a prayer for a peaceful tomorrow. Ellen knows the power of mountain spirituals. She understands the new energy her gospel songs bring to her work-worn brethren, and because she loves them as she loves her music she can bring them with little effort to a communion with their God.

Hillybilly religion means joy, motion, fervent and sometimes fitful prayers for salvation, and untold agony in the death of loved ones. It means coming together after a hard week's labor to visit neighbors, the grown folks sharing the news of the community and the young folks exchanging glances that promise continued social activity in the community, and the babies playing all around, their romping and laughter their special kind of prayer. And, hillbilly religion means salvation from the dreadful specter of life; a new life in tomorrow's land.

At night, when Ellen Rector meditates in prayer, she will thank God for salvation, she will ask that He somehow find a way to make the world a happy place, full of peace and joy like she feels in church, and goodwill to mankind. And if He should not will it so, perhaps He will see her through the hardships of life on earth until He meets her at heaven's door. For that is what hillbilly religion is all about.

We've had eleven funerals right here in Hancock County in the last two weeks. It's more than we ever had before right close together like that. There was seven killed here last Tuesday morning. Then last Saturday evening, there was four more killed—all in car wrecks. And I've been so nervous all weekend I can hardly stand it. My son-in-law-to-be was killed in one of them wrecks.

I have seven children living and three dead. After my fourteen-year-old boy got killed, I stayed worried for a long time. He hadn't joined the church yet, although he'd been saved, and I worried about that till it was about to kill me. I've been taught all my life that if you didn't make a change you'd be lost. He had made his profession but he hadn't been baptized. So I kept praying and praying for the Lord to show me whether he was lost or not. Well, one night about three weeks after he died, I was laying in bed a-prayin', just meditating quietly in prayer, and after a few minutes I just lost sight of everything. I thought I was standing out there in the yard. There was this stairway in front of me, a golden stairway. I looked up the stairs and on the top step I could see my son standing there. He had on the same clothes he was wearing when he was killed, overall pants and a little checkered shirt. He was standing on that top step with a big bright light behind him and I could see him just as plain . . . He was reaching back down with both hands and I heard him say, "C'mon, Mommy . . ." And I walked up to the third step in that stairway before I come back down to reality. And all that worry left me . . .

There is a lot of people that you can't make understand what it means to be saved. The way we've always been taught, we're saved before we've been baptized. But we don't join the church till we know we're ready. Then we get baptized.

When I was fifteen, I felt that I was accountable. I

come to that stage in my life that I knew if I should die, I'd be lost. So it kept troubling me till I couldn't eat nor I couldn't sleep. So that Sunday evening, I'll never forget it, it was the fourteenth day of February, and I was just so troubled I couldn't stand it. I asked the people at church that evening to pray for me. We prayed for hours and hours until everything around me was . . . I mean, I just went out. I couldn't hear anything, I couldn't see anything, I was out like I was in a coma. I lost sight of everything. When I came back to where I was, I had left the bench where I was on my knees and I was in the other side of the room. I done that not even knowing it. And all of that burden, all of that load was gone and I just felt like flying away.

The day I was baptized . . . ohhh, that was the greatest experience I've ever been through. I can remember it. It was in November and ice was froze on the water in the river. We had to break it to get down in there. But it didn't feel cold after I was in the water, it didn't feel cold. I had on a blue skirt and a white blouse. They led me right out in the water and folded my hands on my bosom. They wet my face with water and the preacher said, "I baptize this, my sister, in the name of the Father, and the Son, and the Holy Ghost." Then he put me under the water and he said, "Amen."

I started out leading the singing in church when I was fifteen and I've kept it up through the years. Now I go everywhere, not just one church. I like to go to a place where I can feel equal, where people don't feel like they're more well off than I am. Course, I have a home church—it's Primitive Baptist and we call it Riverside.

There's a whole group of us that goes together and sings at different churches in the community. Henry Bunch, he's got a quartet, and I sing a lot by myself. Then I got two nieces that sings with me in a trio and a nephew and his wife that sings together. And every Saturday night we have a singing at some church or the other.

There was one time when I was singing . . . I was in the church and this song just came to me and, as the Bible says, my cup just run over, and I was up and all over the place before I knew what I was doing. Everybody seemed to be so happy that day. When it hits me like that I don't know it's coming. Then I'm up and gone before I know it. It hits me pretty often. And if you fall, it don't hurt you, no. I've fell lots of times. The spirit'll just hit you until you just black out. Sometimes, when we're really having a good meeting, a lot of the people they just fall out, out maybe for fifteen minutes, just like they're dead. But we most of the time just leave them layin' where they fall. When they come back to, they get up by theirselves.

In the Primitive Baptist church, we do pray the prayer of Faith sometimes when it's necessary. Sometimes the person is healed and sometimes they aren't. It's just according to how much faith they've got in the person making the prayer. If you're sick and if it's not sickness unto death, you can be healed. In some cases, even people with cancer have been healed. Over in Kentucky, they prayed for a woman who had cancer of the stomach. They was holiness people and they prayed for her and anointed her with oil and laid hands on her, and before she left the church, she vomited that thing up. Right there at the church. The Lord does things like that to cause other people to have more faith.

Well, I was healed once like that. It was at a Colored church. They weren't Primitive Baptist, they were holiness. And they were all Colored. There was something wrong with me, I don't know yet just what it was. I was hurting inside till, oohhh, I just couldn't stand it. I went to this Colored church and told them what all I thought was wrong. And I asked them to pray for me. And when they put that oil on my head and laid their hands on my head, I felt that hurting, it come all the way up through me and it went out the top of my head. I never did feel it any more. It never did come back.

One time I was at a tent meeting at Harlan, Kentucky, and there was a holiness preacher there. Well, they brought in a little boy, about twelve years old. And he had a big knot about the size of a golf ball on his leg. They stood him up on the bench there right where everyone could see him. And they prayed for him and anointed him with that oil and they rubbed their hands over that knot. The preacher prayed for him three times. The last time he prayed and rubbed his hand over that knot, that knot went away. I seen it just disappear. Then they was really having a time. They went to talking in other tongues and all.

The Primitive Baptists don't speak in other tongues, though I do believe there is such a gift. And sometimes in our church we have healings, only we don't anoint with oil like the holiness.

The Primitive Baptists, we take the bread and the wine,

and we wash feet. The pastor of the church, he'll pray and tell all members to examine theirselves and see if they're worthy of this, the sacrament service. If they feel like they're worthy, it's passed around by the deacons of the church. The women of the church bake the bread; it's made out of flour and water only, and it's hard, like a biscuit. And they cut it up in little tiny blocks. Each person gets one little block of bread and one sup of wine. The wine tastes like grape juice. Well, that's a spiritual service.

When we go to washing feet, most of the time we just shout and everybody gets happy and runs all over the church house. I've seen them step in the pans of water and turn them over and everything.

The way we wash feet, the women washes the women's feet and the men washes the men's. So we set two benches, one facing the other. The women gets on the benches facing one another and they have the pan of water. They start at the end of the bench. Like me and you sits facing each other at the end of the bench, why, I wash your feet and you wash mine. And we have a towel that we keep around our waist. When I dry your feet, I take off the towel and give it to you and you tie it around your waist. Then you wash mine and use the towel to dry mine and then you pass it on to the woman beside of you. Then, when the women are done, the men do the same way.

For me, it's never been just a habit, going to church. I go because I want to, and I pray every day. I don't pray at no certain time. Well, you don't have to get down on your knees to pray. I work and pray at the same time.

Ellen Rector is a community organizer. She has helped to organize a health clinic where the adults in rural Sneedville can get physical examinations and the children can get measles shots. She also organized a clothing store in Sneedville which is owned and operated by poor people in Hancock County.

I see my work with people as a part of my serving God. I just want to be a help to someone, like helping people here get the health care they need.

We're trying to get ourselves organized here, the poor people, through community meetings. Sometimes our meetings will last for two or three hours, everybody talking about their problems. Our meetings aren't run by any certain person, we just set a time to meet and the meeting is run by the whole community. We've got ourselves named the "Poor People's Organization."

Some of the women in the county that draws welfare, they have a guardian. One woman that draws welfare, she went to her guardian and told him she needed a mattress, that her kids' mattress had just rotted through and she just had to have a new one. He wouldn't give her the money to go buy it herself. He took it on hisself, went to Knoxville, told her he could get it cheaper for her there. So he went and got a mattress and he brought it back and he took it to his home and put it on his bed, and then he gave her his old mattress he'd used for six, seven year.

The guardian gets their check and they're supposed to see after what the people on welfare need. Mostly, the guardians is the ones that owns the stores. Then the women have to beg for what they can get. The welfare department decides who don't know how to manage their own business and appoints them a guardian. If there's a woman that's got maybe two or three children, that's not married, then they appoint her a guardian. They think she's not capable of doing her shopping. Then, when winter comes and she can't get coal, she has to cry for coal, you know what I mean . . .

We have a few merchants around here that's just dirty. When a family that don't know no better comes in to the markets to get their fruits and vegetables from some of these merchants, they load the family up with all the bad food that's kept off the shelf, the kind you and me wouldn't take for nothing.

We're about to open a cannery for every poor family in the county to use. And we're going to provide the seeds for growing their own fruits and vegetables.

Whenever I can, I like to visit people in their homes and do what I can to help them, if it's nothing more than comfort them when they're sick. I just like to help people, help them to feel better.

There are some poor Black people living in and around Hancock County, Tennessee, but most of them are not of the Negro race. They are called Melungeons and are believed to be at least part Indian.

No one really knows where Melungeons first came from, but there have been many guesses. One theory holds that Melungeons are Portuguese immigrants, another that they are of French descent, and the latest theory is that Melungeons are of Jewish origin and came from somewhere around the Mediterranean Sea.

Wherever Melungeons first came from, they have not been treated well since they settled in Eastern Tennessee. They are some of the most oppressed people in this country. Melungeons are dark-skinned like the Negro race and have features similar to the American Indians. Like Negros and Indians, the Melungeon people have been treated as fourth-class citizens of this country.

It is interesting that the poor White people of Eastern Tennessee were first to recognize the equality of Melungeons. When Ellen Rector began organizing poor people in Hancock County, she worked with both poor Whites and Melungeons.

I visit the Melungeons. I've been to their homes to visit them in my work. And they come to our community meetings. Melungeons are what you call twixt and 'tween. They're probably some kind of Indian race. They've been around here all my life and I guess a long time before that. They don't talk exactly like we do, but they're real good to talk up at our meetings. I don't hardly know who is a Melungeon around here. They've about called us all Melungeons. What ain't called Melungeons is called hillbillies . . .

Now, a Strike Is Rough, All the Way Around

BERNICE RATCLIFF
AND LORINE MILLER

MCCAYSVILLE, GEORGIA   ASKA, GEORGIA

*For ten long years we've worked in here since Levi's come to
     town,*
Production keeps on going up, our wages stay low down.
*Let the bosses flash their Yankee smiles and make their hillbilly
     jokes,*
We're walking out at one o'clock, four hundred angry folks.

There are few places as beautiful as North Georgia. The Blue
Ridge Mountains, rolling south from the Smokies, are covered
with mountain laurel and longleaf pine from ridge to ridge.
On the highways, giant logging trucks loaded with timber cut
from the National Forests strain in low gear along the steep
grades, on their way to the sawmills and pulpwood yards that

dot the countryside. There are still deer and wild turkey in the forests, and native trout in the high mountain creeks that can only be reached by foot.

It is a rich land, but the home of poor people. Fannin County, less than one hundred miles north of Atlanta, borders the Tennessee and North Carolina lines. It has few paved roads, no hospital, and the highest taxes in the state. It also has a long and bitter history.

The first residents of Fannin County, the Cherokee Indians, were rounded up at gunpoint in 1836 and force-marched to Oklahoma. During the Civil War, Confederate and Union sympathizers shot and killed each other in ambush in these mountains. For years Fannin County was the only Republican county in the state of Georgia, the heritage of the large number of mountain families who sided with the Union during that war.

In the 1930s, union copper miners in McCaysville, Georgia, and Copperhill, Tennessee, fought a bitter struggle against the Tennessee Copper Company—now owned by Cities Service Corporation—the area's largest single employer, with over two thousand people on its payroll.

Between Aska community, where Lorine Miller lives, and McCaysville, which is Bernice Ratcliff's hometown, lies the mountain town of Blue Ridge, the county seat, and a growing center of the textile industry. The long history of struggle in the county has had its influence on this growth.

In 1966, workers at the Levi-Strauss plant, angered at the failure of the company and their union to honor seniority rights, walked out en masse. For fourteen months the strikers, primarily women, stayed on the picket lines, supported by the earnings of other strikers who went to work at neighboring textile mills. Bernice Ratcliff and Lorine Miller were among those factory workers who walked the picket lines during that wildcat strike.

LORINE: In September of 1964, we got the union in at Levi's. We didn't have much trouble getting the union organized, but some of the girls who worked there just flat out wouldn't sign union cards. The supervisors and the manager threatened a lot of girls, told them they would lose their jobs if they tried to bring a union into Levi's.

BERNICE: The union came about because a lot of our men are union at the Copper Company. The men got to talking with their wives and they all decided Levi's would be a better place to work if we got a union in there.

The girls would go home at night and complain to their men about their rights being violated on the job. If you was a little late to work, or if you had sickness in the family, some of the supervisors wasn't too nice about it. And some of the girls just couldn't hold their production.

We figured if we got a union in there we could get the production lowered. On some of the jobs the production was so high you just couldn't make it. Some girls could make a little money and others made nothing. Levi's set the production by the highest operator, the fastest one.

Well, let's say I was working on the serger machine. Where I might could set on that machine for six months and learn it, it might take another girl nine months to learn it. Some girls can run one machine better than they can run another. But if you didn't make it on the machine they put you on, you went out the door. They didn't give you a chance to try another type of machine.

And you had to keep up that production. You had to be a hundred per cent at least five days out of the week. If you was one hundred and fifty per cent two days running and less than a hundred the other three, it didn't make no difference. If you wasn't a hundred per cent each day you went out the door. They was paying us a dollar and twenty-five cents an hour. That was minimum wage then.

LORINE: What they're supposed to do in a factory is take the fastest operator and the slowest operator on a certain machine and set the production rate somewhere in between theirs, somewhere a little below the fastest so that a normal hand could reach it. But at Levi's they take the fastest worker who's been on the machine the longest and set the rate by her work. They say they lower it but they don't.

Well, the union was voted in two-to-one, and a half-baked contract was written up. Everything in that contract said, "In the opinion of the management . . ." you could have your rights. As long as the *management* agreed with what your rights were. That was the whole contract between International Ladies' Garment Workers Union and Levi-Strauss—"In the opinion of the management."

We knew we had to have a contract, but it was all new to us. We didn't know what to look for in a union contract. A lot of us knew it was a weak contract but we figured we could hold out and get something better later.

But, when the contract says you have to go by the opinion of the management, you *know* the union isn't going to back you.

Well then, we had our union. Then after the first year, renewal time rolled around. There was something in the contract that said if you wanted to pull out after the first year you could do it. So this supervisor comes around and he says to all of us, "Well, this is the time to pull out, girls." I thanked him kindly for coming around, told him I sure did appreciate him telling us. And some of the girls did pull out of the union because they were threatened with losing their jobs. Then August of 1966 came around and a rumor spread that the Company was going to "help" the girls that was making production.

BERNICE: They were trying to say, "You're better off being a Company fan than a union fan . . ."

The Company was going to "help" us by putting in new machines. Only they weren't going to let us run them. They were going to hire new girls for the new machines and lay some of the older workers off. They were going to put the machines in one by one, thinking we wouldn't notice what they was doing. Levi's knew that any of us girls that had worked on the inseam line for some time could operate this new inseam machine, make good production and make some money.

It was an easy machine to run. They knew we could sit down at that machine and just go to sewing and we'd have it made. But the management said they was going to hire a new girl for this machine. And we wanted to know why. So we called a meeting with the manager.

Management had a feeble explanation for the women. They told the workers that "you can't teach an old dog new tricks," and the manager informed the women that Levi's would hire new girls for the new machines because new girls would be easier to train than the veterans of the sewing factory.

The manager went on to explain that not only would the old workers not be given a chance to operate the new machine and make more money, but they would be transferred from their present jobs to replace some of their fellow workers who would be laid off. Then, he explained, Levi's could make more money.

The women told management they would not accept Levi's plan, which was in fact a plan to turn over their employment, to lay off women who were struggling to make production, to switch women who were making production, and to deny the workers their seniority rights. The women told management they would not take other women's jobs nor would they allow new workers to take their jobs. Management reluctantly agreed the women were right and promised to put one of them at the new machine.

The day came when the new inseam machine was to get its first operator. The women came to work on the morning shift wondering if management would keep its promise. They punched in at the time clock and went to their machines. Everyone's eyes were on the shiny new sewing machine, its vacant seat waiting for an operator. The women began to sew on their old machines, but kept sharp eyes on the new piece of equipment.

All at once a Company supervisor appeared in the sewing

room and placed herself standing behind the vacant seat. Then in came a new girl, wide-eyed and nervous about her new job, not knowing she was about to trigger one of this country's most famous textile strikes. Having no idea why all the women were staring at her, the new girl sat down at the new machine and began to sew in the protective shadow of the supervisor.

The women were furious. Management had not kept its promise. Workers crowded into the manager's office demanding an explanation. He had none and the women gave him an ultimatum: give them their new machine or face a walkout of union workers. Then the women went back to work.

BERNICE: When we got back to our machines, the other girls in the plant wanted to know what was happening. We told them and they all said they'd back us up. Then the boss told us to get to work. We wasn't allowed to get up and get a spool of thread or talk to anybody. The supervisors and the bundle boys walked the aisles continuously. Up and down, up and down. They didn't leave the inseam line for a minute.

At twelve o'clock we went to lunch. The union leaders said for us to return to our machines at the first whistle, and then, if they hadn't taken the new girl off that machine, that at the second whistle, five minutes later, we should up and walk out. So we went back to our machines when the first whistle blew. Well, I sat at my machine fiddling with a repair and waiting for the second whistle.

I thought just the inseam line was going to walk out, just us women that were directly affected by the new machine. When the second whistle went off, I reached for my pocketbook, then I looked up and I seen the lower end of the building start out. And I thought, well where are *they* going? I was sitting there amazed, it looked like everybody was a-walkin' out. I just sat there and stared. I was froze to my chair. Then all of a sudden somebody was saying, "Well, come on, Bernice, come *on* . . ." and I finally got up then and walked out.

By then the whole building was empty. Almost five hundred women walked out all together. Here comes the supervisor up and down, here come the bundle boys, here comes the manager. His face was so red it looked like the blood was fixing to come from it. I heard one of them on the phone calling "Big Daddy." The manager saw me and another girl and he wanted to know what we were doing in the place. We said we was just putting in our time sheets so we'd get paid. He shouted, "Well, hurry up and get out of here!"

LORINE: It looked like waves coming out of the building, waves of women moving out of that factory. When we got outdoors, we all went over to the side of the road. Big Daddy had come by then and he come along and said, "You girls get back up here! Let's have a meeting and get this settled." We didn't go back up there. Just about the whole factory was out. There was one or two men that stayed in the cutting room and one man stayed in the shipping room and a few operators stayed at their machines. Levi's had about five hundred workers and when we walked out we left them with about sixty people, counting supervisors, office help, and all.

I stayed out there until eleven o'clock that night. When the night shift came in we started signing them up in the union. The union leaders stayed there all night waiting for a union official to come. When he finally got there we all had a meeting and he made a big speech about us going back to work. Then, after he made that speech, he passed through the crowd patting us on the back and spread the word among the girls that we should just lay with it, that the wildcat *was* really the right thing to do. But he did that quietly. I don't guess the union would have liked that.

For three days and nights the union women picketed out in front of the Levi-Strauss plant in Blue Ridge, Georgia. Then Levi's got a court injunction prohibiting the women from picketing more than two at a time. The women set their base of operations up the road a few hundred yards from Levi's gate, built themselves a tiny wooden shack, put a fire in a trash bin to keep warm, and began walking a picket line which did not break up for fourteen months.

Meanwhile, Levi's hired scab workers to replace the women. Georgia law is made for the benefit of industry, not for the workers, and "open shop" rulings make it difficult to carry out an effective strike. And so Levi's continued to sew their blue jeans while the striking women went hungry because the union they had joined refused to aid them in their wildcat strike.

The union men at Tennessee Copper Company came to the aid of their women. Out of their strike fund the men donated three thousand dollars to an emergency relief fund for the women. This allowed women who were the sole supporters of their families to buy enough food to feed their families during the first months of the strike, and paid women for walking the picket line according to their need.

But the money was soon spent and the women had to find another way to keep the picket line moving out in front of Levi's. Some women went to work in other sewing factories in the area and gave part of their earnings to the strike fund. The other sewing companies supported Levi's management, however, and if they caught a woman giving part of her paycheck to the strike fund she was fired.

Other women spent their time walking the picket line. One woman was knocked down by a car driven into the factory yard by a Company scab. And while Lorine Miller walked the picket line wearing a sign around her neck, she had that sign knocked about more than once.

The Company tried desperately to settle the strike because they soon found that scab labor was not skilled enough to run their sewing machines. Their theory about training new women proved wrong when they were faced with training some four hundred new sewing operators.

LORINE: One day Big Daddy came down to the gate while I was picketing and he walked the line for about an hour and a half. He was trying to convince me to go back in to work. They had been hiring scabs but they couldn't find experienced workers like us to run the machines.

Big Daddy told me if I came back in to work he would see that I got my machine and my seniority back. I said, "Well, I don't think you've ever done it before and I don't think you'll do it now." "And," I said, "if you don't want to bury me, you better stop those girls up there.

Those office girls come driving out of your yard pretty fast." He said, "Well, you're not supposed to be walking back and forth across the road." I said, "Well, what good would it do to walk *up* and *down* the road? I want the work in your factory stopped and that's the reason I'm blocking your gate by going back and forth. And, one more thing," I said, "the very next time I see a girl drive out of there barreling at us pickets, I'm going to bash her car when it comes at us." Well, they sort of slowed down after that.

During the strike there was some violence. There was a house burned down and a few houses and cars shot into. But the gunshots into the houses and cars, I didn't agree with that. Now, into an empty car, I don't disagree with that. But in a house, most of the time there are people inside with children and you don't know what you'll hit when you shoot into a house.

They dynamited a couple places down towards Ellijay. Both sides were using these tactics, but the local union people didn't plan ours. They were planned by outsiders, men who came from other places to help us on the strike. And the dynamite was their idea. It's not a woman's style to destroy like that. Women aren't the ones who get out with a gun and go hunting anybody.

Now, a strike is rough, all the way around. I don't believe in going behind someone's back and shooting them or dynamiting a house where there might be children inside. But, now, if we could have took baseball bats and gone in there and faced those women that was taking our machines, taking our jobs, why I would've led the party. I told one of the girls, "Let's go in there and clean that bunch out," and that's what I would have done if I'd had my way.

BERNICE: Now, to pull hair, or to tear those machines up, I would have loved that. Walk right up to them, don't go behind their backs.

As rough as the strike became for the women, the ILGWU never came to their aid. The union which advertises itself in *Ms.* magazine as being a union that works for working women, ignored the pleas of almost five hundred Blue Ridge Mountain women who were dues-paying ILGWU members. The ILGWU stuck to the "Sweetheart" contract they had with Levi-Strauss and called the women's wildcat strike "illegal."

LORINE: Well, I don't understand unions. And I seriously doubt if I'll ever join another one again, unless I go to work in a closed shop. I'm afraid nobody ever took the time to explain unions to me.

BERNICE: Well, *I'll* tell you about a union. You know what's true, if a union is run and run by the *people* it would be a fine thing. But it's money; if the union gets a little money to go along with management, then the leaders will accept that money and then you and me are left holding the bag. And that's what ILGWU did to us.

After a year and two months of picketing, the time came for contract renewal between ILGWU and Levi-Strauss. The scab workers, not the union women on the picket line, were allowed to vote for or against the union. The union was voted out and the long strike came to an end. The women knew they had lost any chance of support from the union. There was no use in holding out on the picket line. They packed up their picket signs, put out the fire and abandoned the little wooden shack they had used for headquarters. They went home and faced their families, defeated victims of the hand-holding textile giants and union officials. They weren't sure what to do next. But one thing was certain: they had to find work.

There are some women who like factory work. They like the feeling of running a sewing machine, seeing piece work eventually turn into finished products. It is hard, physical work, but under the right conditions many women enjoy it. Some of the women in the Blue Ridge strike felt that way.

Not long after the strike ended, a few women who had walked the picket line decided to start their own sewing factory. They wanted to own, manage, and operate a work-place where the women in Fannin County, Georgia, could work without unfair production rates, without the tension and tedium which are day-to-day factors in the lives of most garment workers. They wanted to make a new kind of fac-tory—the kind that did not exist in this country. And they did it.

For six years there has been a factory operating in Fannin County, Georgia, that puts Levi-Strauss to shame. The fac-tory is owned, managed, and operated by women who led the Blue Ridge strike. In fact, the working conditions in the women's factory are so good that many women are leaving Levi-Strauss and coming to work at McCaysville Industries.

At McCaysville Industries, the women sew uniforms, the

kind nurses and restaurant workers and beauticians wear. Their quality is so superb that they have sewn for such well-known clothes merchants as J. C. Penney's.

When you walk into McCaysville Industries, you get a feeling of women working together. The workers in the factory are happy. That is the most unusual thing about this worker-run factory.

Everyone in the factory is treated equally. The women are paid on a production basis. Because they are allowed to work at their own rate of speed, the women are not nervous and can produce much more and make more money than they did under the tense conditions at Levi's.

A woman is given time off if she is sick or if she needs to see a doctor or has family problems. If a woman needs to go to the bathroom or wants to take a cigarette break, she can do it without the fear of being penalized by a supervisor. When their children get out of school for the day they can come by the factory and wait for their mothers. Husbands often come by the factory and sit at their wives' machines, talking for five or ten minutes. And, from a record player in the back of the sewing room, country music floats through the building, making it altogether a pleasant place to work.

The women of the Blue Ridge strike had a real kind of victory. They have successfully removed themselves from the oppressive conditions created by the giant textile corporations and have created a new kind of factory. They have often been criticized by people in the garment industry for not "running a tighter ship" and for not being "business-like." But they founded their factory on the belief in the dignity of working people and, profit or loss, the women who sit behind the sewing machines will always come first.

My Grandpa Always Taught Me to Fight

SHIRLEY SOMMEROUR
AURARIA (KNUCKLESVILLE), GEORGIA

The bosses breathe right down your neck, they spit right in your
  eye,
Before you're half a lifetime old you're tired enough to die.
Well, I am a hard-working girl, I've been so from my birth,
I want to go to heaven, cause it sure is hell on earth.

Auraria, Georgia, isn't on any maps. Like many communities in the Southern Appalachians, it is little more than a wide place in the road. There are a few houses, some vacant and some occupied, and an old general store building, its boards weathered to a dull gray and its Coca-Cola signs almost consumed by rust.

There is little at the dusty crossroads to suggest that in the early 1800s this now vacant place was the site of one of the largest and most prosperous communities in the Georgia mountains. The area housed some four hundred families, drawn there by this country's first gold rush.

Dug out of the ground and panned from the creeks that drain the Blue Ridge, the gold was melted down and coined at the U. S. Mint in Dahlonega, some six miles to the north. From as far away as Copperhill, Tennessee, mule-drawn wagons came each week to carry back the gold coins to make the payroll at the copper mines, an empty safe sitting in the middle of the wagon, the gold hidden under a pile of dirty feedsacks in a corner.

The prospector who first struck gold at Auraria, George Sommerour, was one of the few who stayed when the rest of the miners set out for California in 1849. His great-granddaughter, Shirley Sommerour, still lives on the edge of the onetime boomtown he helped to found.

At one time Auraria was better known for gold than even California. The way our family story goes, there was three brothers come here. But they was all called by a different name because nobody could ever seem to say it right. One of these three brothers was my grandfather's father. He stopped in Auraria. Then one of them went up to Amicalola Falls and the other went on up toward Cleveland, Georgia. And every one of them finally settled their name to be Sommerour.

That was my maiden name. It has to be. I don't have a father.

My grandfather was the biggest prospector around here. Over at Blackburn State Park, they have my grandfather's old homeplace there. People's been from all over the United States to talk to him about where the gold was.

Grandpa and Grandma raised me after they raised fourteen children of their own. The woods was my playground. I lived there with my grandpa. But to actually remember a father . . . my grandpa was the only father I've ever known. And my grandmother raised me and she was the only real mother I've ever known. I used to go out in the woods around Grandpa's house and collect flowers.

Right next to the house was the family graveyard and it was my job to keep it up. Before it became the family graveyard, there was all kinds of people buried there. There was slaves buried in there, all kinds of people. I used to go out and clean up the graveyard, set back up the stones that had tilted, and pick wild violets.

One time, somebody tried to rob a grave down there. They had dug way down and just about reached the casket when we caught them. Grandpa got the shotgun, went out there and run them off. So we filled it up and set the stone back on it. There was no marking on the stone. It was just an old brown rock.

My mother was fifteen when she had me. Then she had another girl before she got married. Now she's married to my stepfather, Major Reeves. He works over there at the Park. Major Reeves had eight children of his own when he married my mother.

I didn't realize I was illegitimate until I was eleven year old. Yet, I had people call me "bastard" and make smart remarks as far back as I can remember, when I was about three, four year old.

I had one aunt who wouldn't come into my grandmother's house unless I wasn't there. Once, I heard her remark that I was the family shame. I couldn't understand it. Grandma would always call me her honey and just let it go.

Back then I didn't realize what the word bastard meant. Children I played with would come and tell me they couldn't play with me no more, their mother didn't allow them to play with people like me. I didn't know what they was talking about. I thought they was just mad at Mama or something.

I had one cousin, he loved to beat me better than anything. He'd beat the fire out of me and call me "bastard," and I still didn't think nothing about it. They'd call me "son-of-a-bitch" and I'd just let it go. But when they started beating on me, I fought back.

My grandpa always taught me to fight. And I didn't take nothin' off of nobody. Me, I fight. When one of my brothers or sisters would pop off at me and call me "little son-of-a-bitch" and "bastard," I'd get in a fight with them. Then my stepfather would beat me.

One time, one of my stepsisters popped off at me and called me "bastard." Well, I beat the tar out of her and threw her down a flight of stairs. And me and her have got along good ever since.

Often rejected by the other children in the neighborhood, Shirley spent a lot of time out on the mountainsides alone, picking wild flowers for the family graveyard. She became independent and adventurous and she was not afraid of the ghosts who traditionally haunt graveyards and old houses.

There's an old houseplace in Auraria that used to belong to my great-grandfather. It had set empty for years about the time I was eight or nine year old. There was pecan trees around the house and just every kind of beautiful flower. I'd go there and collect flowers all the time. I knew just when each flower would be blooming.

Well, everybody would talk about this house being haunted. They could hear chains, they could hear cries and moaning . . . Well, I'd been in that house a million times, never heard a sound. I'd be down there by myself just picking flowers and I never did hear a sound.

One day I took my brother down there with me. We was picking daffodils. We piddled around, oh, I'd say a good hour. Then he commenced to running on the porch and yelling. I had always been quiet down there. I told him, "Ronnie, be *quiet*." He said, "Why?" I said, "I don't know, it's just a feeling I have. We should be quiet or we'll bother somebody." He laughed at me and he just jumped off the porch and screamed right out loud. And you never heard the likes of chains in your life. And somebody just a-moanin' and a-groanin'. We both heard it . . . he run and left me standing there. So I caught him, brought him back and made him stand there while I went inside the house to search. I went all through the house a-searchin', couldn't find anything. It was just as quiet as it could be. Well, I come on outside, got up the rest of my flowers, and everything was quiet. So Ronnie got a little braver. He walked up to the house, grabbed and put a hand on the porch. And when he did, the chains and everything started again. The awfulest screams you ever heard in your life.

We went on home and told Grandpa. I told Grandpa, "Ronnie done it. He bothered someone." Well, he laughed at me. But I kept going down there after flowers by myself, and I was always real quiet and I never heard nothing.

Then come summertime and Ronnie went back down there with me one day. We were picking a red flower that grows on a tree with thorns. Well, Ronnie started talking. He walked up to the house, set down on the porch, and started a-badgerin' me about picking the flowers. He wouldn't pick them cause they had thorns. And just as soon as he started talking, seemed like the house heard his voice. It cut loose again. He refused to go back there with me after that.

Soon after that, my aunt and her husband, they moved into this old house. Nothing actually happened there as long as their children was quiet. But when they got noisy, it seemed like the house would react.

One day when I was about nine year old, me and my cousin and a couple others was running around and playing in the room right off to the side of the porch. There was little shelves all around the room and it had a solid roof. There was one little hole in the corner of the roof and it had planks in it.

Well, we was running around and a-climbin'. I climbed up on this shelf and started to fall. I reached right to those planks to catch myself. And when I did, a little door opened. There was a room up there.

I looked in. Paul said, "What do you see?" I said, "A bed. A straw bed." He said, "You see a *what?*" "A bed." Oh, he just badgered the fool out of me. I said, "Well, damn it, I see a bed. There's some clothes, too." So they dared me and I went climbing on up into this little loft. Here comes Paul and the others behind me.

We was all up there and got to looking at the coat. There was blood on it, and there was a hole through it. And on the straw bed, there was blood all over it. And there was some chains laying there. They was rusted and it looked like blood on them. It was a Confederate coat and it had stripes on the arm.

We brought the coat back to Grandpa and showed it to him. He never would answer our questions about the house. He made us burn the coat, made us take the bed down and burn it. And he took the chains and throwed them away. Then, after two days of bothering him about it, I got him to tell me the story.

Grandpa set me down and told me this story: There was a Confederate soldier, he was wounded. And he was being hunted. Well, he came to the house and asked my people to hide him there. And they put him up in this room and fixed him a bed. He was wounded so bad . . . they did everything they could to save his life. The soldier was almost dead when the men that was hunting him come to the house. The soldier moaned and they heard the noise and they found him up there. The men were wrapping chains all around him to drag him back and my people told them, "The man's dying, leave him be." And the men laughed at my people. But the soldier died before they could get him down out of that loft. One of the men went over to the soldier and kicked him. Then they just took some sort of identification off of him and went away.

My people took the chains off his body and took his body out and buried it right near the house. One woman who was there when they buried him swears she could hear him cry when they was a-movin' the body to bury it. He was a young boy, Grandpa said, he wasn't no more than a kid. They closed the door to the loft and left everything there like it was when he died.

I go down there lots. And I think to myself, I'd just

like to know where they buried him. I'd like to find the grave and fix it up for him.

Religion has affected Shirley Sommerour's life in many ways. And, like so many other communities, Auraria learned that religion is only as honest as the preacher.

I went to the Primitive Baptist church, was a regular member since I was three or four year old. I was "saved" when I was seven year old. I was baptized when I'd just hit eight. The preacher had to baptize me twice. Claims he slipped on a stone and fell the first time. Well, then he had to go back for seconds and try it again. He got me under that time. I always did wonder why he had to put me under twice.

I went to church every Wednesday and Sunday nights for years. Then they got a "differences of opinion" in our "holy" church about what preacher they was going to elect. The differences was so great they had to get up one night in the middle of a service and have a fist fight. I got up and walked out.

There was a man come here to preach, and he told the people he just couldn't preach in that little old white church up on the mountain. So he run around the community doing everybody dirty, got all the money he could from people. Then he had the mountain dozed down flat and built him a big brick church to preach in.

One time he preached my cousin into hell. Come over to my cousin's house one Saturday night and my cousin was there with a beer setting next to him. The preacher asked him to come to church the next morning. Well, the next day my cousin was driving right down this road here and he had a heart attack. Run off the road and was dead before he ever hit.

The preacher was the first to come along. He didn't offer to go down and get him out of the car to see if he was even alive. Then come a couple cars of people and they run down there to check on him. The preacher told them they was going to hell, he raised heck with them for touching the body, told them their hands was unclean and God would punish them.

The day of the funeral, after the two preachers got through, he got up, and he wasn't even asked by the family to preach. He said that anybody who'd drink, not come to church, be out clowning in a car, was going to hell. He said that Burel was going to hell. Then he said it was the sum of our upbringing that made the people around here that way. He made a community of enemies that day.

Then the preacher decided it wasn't good enough for him here and now he's off at Emory University getting a college degree. We later found out he wasn't a preacher at all, just a boy who was going to college near here. The people of this congregation paid for his college education.

Shirley finished the eighth grade in school. When she was fourteen she was married. She had two children the year she was fifteen. Her first baby died at birth and is buried at her grandfather's feet in the family cemetery. Divorced now, and the mother of two girls, Shirley makes the family living like everyone else in Auraria at the mill.

"The mill" is the Pine Tree plant of Lees Carpets, a division of the gigantic Burlington Industries, Inc. Over a thousand North Georgians work at the mill, which runs twenty-four hours a day, fifty-one weeks out of the year, spinning the yarn which will go into luxury carpets.

There are no suburbs in Lumpkin County, and when the folks who live there talk about setting down rugs in their small houses and trailers, they are talking about linoleum, which sells for about twenty cents a square foot. No one is getting rich in the mill. Women like Shirley, who work three weeks out of six on the 11 P.M. to 7 A.M. graveyard shift, are lucky to bring home sixty dollars a week. Their "fringe benefits" include impaired hearing from the constant noise, respiratory problems caused by dust and gas, hypertension resulting from the high-speed, dangerous machinery, and the drugs many of them take in order to keep going. Like the luxury carpets which Burlington sells, they are walked on constantly.

I went to work at Pine Tree Carpet Mills when I'd just hit my nineteenth birthday. We don't make carpets, we make the yarn for carpets. I work in doubling and twisting. We twist the yarn on cones and it's shipped out of here to places like Canton, Georgia.

There's no place in the mill to move away from the dust. They got air hoses in there to move the dust, but it just made more dust for us to breathe off. Now they stopped that cause it was making our eyes go bad.

Lately, the bosses have been showing a lot of interest to the walls in the mill. Where before there was a lot of skim of dust on the walls, now they're having someone to come up and wipe them off and wash them so they look real good.

One thing that happens in the mill is women are getting a lot of gas from the tow machines where the men are operating machines run on butane gas. Women that sits behind these machines have almost passed out from the gas those machines throw off. That gas is bad. It burns us in our eyes and we have to breathe it in, yet we still need those tow machines.

Lately the women in the mill have been talking about the noise. None of us that's worked there for some time can hear as well as we used to. It's impaired our hearing so bad, we go home and have to turn everything up loud so's we can hear it. It really has made our hearing worse.

There's about a thousand women in all that works in the mill, including all three shifts. We work on a rotating system. For two weeks we'll go in on the night shift. Then we'll switch to the day shift and then to the evening shift. It's been that way since the mill opened. Once you get used to it, it's not so bad, but sometimes it can be hard. Like, if you're on the night shift, you sleep in the evening, get up around eleven at night and face a plate of beans. Well, beans don't look so good when you just wake up. And a egg don't look so good that time of night either. So in some ways it's kindly hard to get adjusted.

There are pills being used by women in the mill. The woman have to use them lots of times cause of the rotating shift and getting used to it. See, they have to keep up their production. So they use the pills to speed them up when they don't feel too good.

The pills can be got by just snapping your fingers. You can get them through the black market here. One pill they use is the "green heart" and another is the "speckled bird." And now there are stronger pills. They got black

RJs and red RJs. Amphetamines. Then there's a little bitty white one.

One time when I was on the night shift after being at a funeral all day, a woman give me a "green heart." She said it wouldn't hurt me and would help me keep up with my work. Well, I didn't really want to, but I took it and I did the best work I've ever done that night. Then another time a woman give me a "speckled bird" and I did real good that night too. The women give them to each other to help each other out.

Once, when I was feeling real bad, a woman come to me with a little bitty white pill. She said it would really speed up my work and make me feel better. Well, I wasn't too sure about the pill so I only took half of it. I got so sick I had to ask to be dismissed from work that night. Then about three weeks later I began having nightmares. I'd see the walls turn into big awful fishes, I'd see the most terrible monsters you'd ever imagined. Later, I found out from a doctor that the little white pill was LSD.

Shirley and the other women at Pine Tree have to meet production every day. If they don't they will be out of a job, and they know what that means. And so rather than face a monthly welfare check, insufficient to feed and clothe their families, and forced to share the financial burden of the family, they work at the mill.

There is no union at Pine Tree and management has done nothing to make working conditions better for their employees. Recently, this division of Burlington issued earplugs and head sets to the mill workers in an effort to meet the requirements of the Occupational Health and Safety Act of

1969. But the ear devices did not help the workers. Many of them have reported that wearing equipment causes extreme nausea and chronic ear bleeding. And, although the walls of the mill are regularly washed to pass inspection by a chance visit from the Occupational Safety and Health Administration, they are the only part of the mill free from masses of lint and dust which the workers still breathe into their lungs.

Management hasn't done anything about the drug problem, either. Many workers believe the company keeps the drug pushers in business; they seem to encourage drug use by the rigid production rate and the rotating shift system they impose on the women. And it does not look like the working conditions at Pine Tree Carpet Mills will change for the better any time soon.

Shirley Sommerour has survived because there was no other choice. Pushed away by her family and community because of her illegitimacy, subjected to some of the worst working conditions in this country today, Shirley has fought back tooth and nail since she was a small girl, relying on the proud traditions of her pioneer grandparents for strength and courage.

The scars do not show on the outside. Good-looking, careful about her appearance, Shirley looks very much like the stars of the Grand Old Opry she sees on her television set. But she will never live in a mansion or drive a Lincoln Continental. Unless conditions change for her and the thousands of women like her, she will spend the rest of her life working for minimum wage in a dusty mill, trying at the same time to remember and to forget how she got where she is.

I'm Proud to Be a Hillbilly

DONNA REDMOND
ATLANTA, GEORGIA

You think that rich and famous
Is all there is to be,
But the working girl don't need that,
All she needs is to be free.

Atlanta, Georgia, is a long way from the small town of Balfour, North Carolina, where Donna Redmond was raised. Born the daughter of Ruby Green, Donna grew up in a little cotton mill town where her mother worked in the mill. After years of trying to make it there, Donna followed in the wake of thousands of other hillbillies and migrated to Atlanta.

Donna Redmond is now a working mother trying to raise two children and support them on the money she makes as a receptionist in a fashionable Atlanta insurance agency. Her life is not really a success story as much as it is a story of necessity. And she has never forgotten where she came from or how she got where she is today.

Donna works for a living because she has to. She is presently the sole supporter of herself and her children, a responsibility she could not meet in a small mountain town. There were no jobs for a woman whose memories of her mother's suffering would not allow her to go to work in a mill, so Donna packed her bags, gathered her children, and drove across the country to the Pacific Northwest in search of decent employment. But all she found was a scarcity of jobs and an intense discrimination against hillbillies. She came back to the mountains and tried again to find work that would pay her enough to raise her family.

For a while, Donna worked in an electronics parts factory in Hendersonville, North Carolina. But the wages were so low she could hardly afford to keep her children in school, and so once again she packed up herself and her children, and drove a U-Haul truck to Atlanta, hoping to make it this time. She found work and she stayed.

The story of Donna's transition is not as important as the attitudes she developed along the way. If her outspokenness about the conditions of working-class women offends some people, it will certainly be applauded by other working-class women. Because Donna Redmond is a feminist in the tradition of the working class.

My mother worked in the cotton mill here, where they made the gauze wrapping for Kotex. And I honest to God never knew they came in boxes. I always thought they came in little individual packages with pins inside.

And your mama always brought them home from work to you, you didn't have to go out and buy those things.

When we were little kids, me and Vince, we had a little glass duck dish that sat on the water heater in the bathroom, and all the Kotex pins went into this little duck dish. On rainy days when we couldn't go outside to play, I would sit and string those pins together.

We used to go all around the house with them. At one point we figured we had five thousand pins. We had pins when we didn't have anything else. Don't worry if you lose a button, we got pins. It was the neighborhood joke. The Corns've got pins.

Mother was a Corn and we lived with her parents. We go way, way back to the first circuit riding preacher that ever came through here, before there was anything but wilderness.

We've always been poor people. My great-grandfather had twelve sons; he was a dirt farmer. My grandfather kidnapped my grandmother at a little country church up on the mountain and took her in a horse and buggy to Greenville, South Carolina, to marry her. She didn't want to go. She was seventeen and he was nineteen. He helped build the railroad that runs through the Green River. Granny cooked for the railroad gang, fixed washpots full of pinto beans, cooked for all those guys and did their laundry.

When Granny was young, she was an orphan and she was shipped out to all these families, packaged off from one to the other when she was like five, six, and seven. There was an old lady up on the mountain. She was known as "T'ain't Sally Jones," and she took in homeless girls and worked them for their room and board. Granny finally wound up with her.

The way this old lady punished these girls if they did anything wrong was to pull the hair at their temples, pull the hair completely out. The girls had to do man's labor, plus the cooking and cleaning.

Granny told me that when she started menstruating, it was in the middle of winter and the snow was real deep. She was down at the stream getting water and it started and the blood was in the snow. She didn't tell T'ain't Sally for about three months because she was scared to death. She thought she was going to die. She didn't know the first thing about it, didn't even know that animals did it. She thought T'ain't Sally would think she'd done something bad or was dying. It took her three months before she got around to telling anybody.

I first learned about sex when I was five years old . . . in the mill town, from my cousin. He took me home with him one day and nobody was there. Everyone was over at my house canning peaches. So, okay. So then his sister, who's like two years older than he is, and he was about ten, she comes in the house and decides she's gonna direct this little thing. And she's got some *really* good ideas about the games we're gonna play. Well, my mother got to looking for me and she found us. We were getting pretty involved there when she found us.

Mama talked to us about sex. I can't remember when she didn't. I think she was unusual in the way she approached it. If we wanted to tell her dirty jokes, we could tell her dirty jokes. If she wanted to tell us a dirty joke, she'd tell us a dirty joke. We didn't get all that cracked up with the other kids cause we could say, ha, ha, my *mother* told me *that* one last week.

Mama set us down and just explained sex to us so there was never any question. She told my brother, "You'll never leave the house without fifty cents in your pocket," and said I would never leave the house without a dime for a phone call. The fifty cents was for him to buy a rubber in case he decided he was going to . . . "Do it, but for *God's sake* . . ."

I started dating when I was twelve. Mama didn't know about it. I was sneaking around with boys who were sixteen and seventeen and had cars. There was a lot of petting going on and I was liking the hell out of it. When I was fourteen, that's when I got my first. After that, it was a downhill drag all the way.

We kept it up, every chance we got . . . back seat of a car . . . that's really a bad scene, you know? Scared all the time. That's when I introduced myself to my mother's douche bag. Didn't know what to do with it exactly, but I figured I'd try it anyway. It scared me to death. I'd do it and go home living in fear. Knowing Mama was going to find out, or I'd get pregnant, or something was going to happen. And it finally happened, I got pregnant.

When I got pregnant, I told the guy it happened with. He told me it was *my* problem and brought me some quinine and sulfate pills. They didn't work. We were having final exams at school and between exams I'd have to go and throw up.

He was from a family that was a lot better off than us. He decided to uphold the family name, *his* family name, to keep everybody from thinking he was a son-of-a-bitch. So he bought me an engagement ring which I couldn't wear cause I hadn't told Mama yet. But I finally had to tell her and that was one of the hardest things I ever had to do.

Mama was cool through the whole thing; taking me to the doctor, finding out I was pregnant for sure. I lied about it to the doctor, told him there was no way, I was still a virgin. I didn't know he could tell. There was no *way* I could lie out of that one.

Mama was understanding. She said, "If you want to go away and have it, fine. If you want to get married, I don't like it but I can't stop you. If you want to stay here, I'll be here, I'll stick it out with you." Okay. I was fifteen years old and three months pregnant. So we got married.

Donna had two children before her marriage finally broke up. While she was still married and raising her babies, Donna managed to get her high school equivalency diploma and then she found a job. She worked for a while at a community action agency where she was one of the few working-class employees in the office. She was also one of the few people in the office able to communicate effectively with poor people and was effective because she talked their language, because she was one of them.

The agency where Donna worked sponsored VISTA (Volunteers in Service for America) workers and Donna came to know the volunteers quite well.

One girl VISTA told me recently that I don't know anything about life because I had never been to college, never been to New York City. Said I didn't know anything about what's *really* going on, like campus riots and all that crap. I may live in my own little world, but as far as knowing anything about life, that's a bunch of bull. Cause you just don't get pregnant, get married at fifteen, get divorced, work to support your kids and yourself without knowing a *little* bit about where it's really at. And I don't care if she *has* hitchhiked all over the country. Anybody that's got damn little enough sense to get out and hitchhike these days ain't too up on what's happening.

I really have this thing with these VISTAs, them coming in here with this idea that we're a bunch of poor ignorant hillbillies. I'm proud to be a hillbilly. And if you don't like the way I talk, then, damn it, go home! And don't make fun of my Southern accent, and if I want to eat grits for breakfast . . . dang straight, I think grits are the greatest thing that come along.

I wonder if these VISTAs ever put the shoe on the other foot and figured if it wasn't for us "poor old ignorant hillbillies" they wouldn't have a damn place to go for them to feel good. But they're gonna make theirselves feel really big. They've all come from upper middle-class families, all had Mama and Daddy handing them everything they ever wanted, ever needed. And as for their college educations, take your college educations and shove it.

Okay. That's great. They come down here and they gonna tell *me* about *poverty?* They tell us they're frustrated, they can't communicate with these people here. *How the hell they gonna communicate with us?* They haven't lived our lives. They don't know what it's about. They want to have "gut feeling." All right then, damn it. Give up Mama and Daddy, don't go back in a year.

Come down here and spend the rest of your life. Forget your college education you got so you could get a good job in some Northern-based plant that's got their little sweatshops down here. Fine. But don't take advantage of cheap mountain labor. Live like the rest of us do.

I don't think anybody who is so hung up with "Who am I, where am I going?" has got any business trying to help somebody else. VISTA: Take a year out from living to decide what you want to do . . . at the expense of the poor people and the taxpayers. What are they going to change anyway? These folks here know who they are and where they're going. Ain't going to go nowhere except where they been for the past sixty years.

I've seen my mama go to work when she wasn't able to walk. She couldn't go to the doctor cause she couldn't spend the money. I've seen her wear the same dress for years, it was the only decent one she had. She had two pair of cut-off blue jeans to wear to work. If being able to work like a horse for a living is being liberated for a woman, I'd just as soon be dependent.

When a woman gets up into a high position in one of these corporations that's oppressing people, she's not going to change things. She's gonna be in the same bag the big-shot men are. All she's doing is making herself feel good, and the more money she earns the better she's gonna feel, and the more people she oppresses is the more money she's gonna get.

I don't want to compete with a man. I don't *have* to compete with a man. I *know* I can do it. As far as taking care of myself and my kids, getting a job, I know I can do that. And, too, the fact that I have a tenth-grade education and I'm not a ding-bat. I didn't have to spend ten thousand dollars to get an education. And when it comes down to talking about living, I can get right in there with the big shots. I may not use ten-dollar words like Germaine Greer to express myself.

It might surprise some folks to hear that hillbilly women are in contact with what's happening in the world. A hell of a lot of us *do* read more than the Sears & Roebuck catalog. We know about Kate Millett, Germaine Greer, Gloria Steinem, and other middle-class bourgeois who put out more talk than do.

There's some kind of courage and independence in a woman who's had to work hard all her life. Like the women around here. Even if you've got a man, it's not easy. The women have to work too, cause they're mostly low-income families. You've got to either do without or go out and help make the money. And I don't think any woman is going to go out and work hard, make a paycheck and keep a job, keep up a home, take care of the kids, do all that at the same time without getting to where she feels pretty damn independent.

Maybe you just get hard. I mean *strong*. But I don't think there are any women around that are more *woman* than hillbilly women. When things aren't like they should be, you don't sit around and cry and say, "I'm frail, I'm soft, I just can't handle it," or sling around ten-dollar words. You just do whatever has to be done.

If I caught a woman messing around with my man, I'd beat the hell out of her. If I wanted him bad enough. And then, if he was cooperating, I'd beat the hell out of him.

In my mind I can't separate women's rights from people's rights. That's what women should be concerned with, is *people's* rights. And if they would get off the kick of jaunting around the world to speak about women's liberation, the kick of becoming famous, and saying, "To hell with men" and "I don't need a man"—that's no different than men saying women are second-rate—that's so much money that's wasted that could really be put to good use. Oh, God, what it could do to help poor people . . . And anyway, all a woman is doing then is admitting she's scared to death of men and not very secure in herself as a woman.

Women are doing it to themselves. They're yapping now about freedom to think, freedom to be themselves. And nobody can give you that. Nobody can make you an individual, give you self-respect. Some of the proudest people in this country are poor people. And I am me and you're not going to shit-can me without me fighting back. Cause I'm worth something even if it's just going to take so many feet to bury me in.

But who can liberate your mind if you can't do it for yourself? When women get hung up on hollering "women's lib" they're overlooking so many other things that have to go with it. Like freeing the Black people, freeing the Chicanos, the Orientals, poor people, whoever . . .

Middle-class women's lib is a trend; working women's liberation is a necessity. Now women have the vote—we still have an oppressive society, we still have wars. It's the society that's oppressing people, the whole setup. And that includes some pretty snobbish women.

Okay. I'm White. If all I have to make me feel better than anybody else is a freak of nature, I ain't got a whole hell of a lot going for me. I'm White, I'm proud to be White. I've got it a whole hell of a lot easier than if I was black, yellow, red, or anything else. But I'm also proud to be a *woman*. I don't want to run a Euclid earth-mover. I just want to be a woman and have a man that has sense enough to treat me like an equal.

I want to look like a woman. And I think damn sure when I wear hot pants you ain't gonna mistake me for a man. What is it? Women have lost their pride in being female. I love makeup, I love perfume and jewelry and frills and lace. I want to look like a woman, I want to smell like a woman, I want to act like a woman.

You always tend to want the things you have the least of. Like the women working in the mills and factories. They want nice things but they've not got the money to get them. If a woman doesn't have the right to look like a woman then she doesn't have any rights.

If a working woman wants curls in her hair, damn sure let her have curls. She hasn't got much else to live for. When you have to go out doing man's work all week, hell, if you want to go blow five dollars in the beauty shop to feel like a woman on the weekend, that's little enough to ask. And if you want a bottle of halfway decent perfume, that's a pretty cheap price to pay for what you have to put up with all week. Now, I *have* smelled some perfumes that would drive a man away. Evening in Paris is a sure killer.

Have you ever thought about this? Working women who work in the mills and factories, they've had the same hairstyle for the past fifteen or twenty years. It's like four rollers on the top, the little curls in front, two little spit curls, and combed away from the face. Every one of them. It may be a variation, but basically it's the same. Why? Why is it only the middle-class and upper middle-class women can afford to go to an expensive beauty shop and get a modern haircut, a style that's really the *in* thing? Yet working women are some of the best-looking women around. Damn straight.

Though she might not admit it, Germaine Greer will agree with me. Like, she puts down makeup and fancy clothes in her book. But after looking at the picture of her on the book's cover, I wonder how many hours she spends at the mirror. Wonder what famous makeup artist showed her how. Or did she just learn like the rest of us deluded females?

Hell, it's part of being a woman to make her man feel like a big man. And that doesn't mean you're his slave. No man feels like a man with a woman who acts and feels inferior to him. Love and sexual gratification depend on both the man and the woman. It takes a good woman to do it, if you've got a good man. So why not make him feel big?

It's just like self-satisfaction and self-gratification with sex. If you're in there just for your own satisfaction, you may as well forget it. Well, if I'm gonna sleep with a guy, I'm gonna let him know I'm the best damn woman he's had in a long time and he's gonna want to come back. And if I'm really interested in a man, I want him to feel like he's the king. It makes me feel gratified to know I'm woman enough to do it. But if I know he doesn't care about my satisfaction, just wants to get his own kicks, that'd turn me off in a minute. And I think you can tell that before you even get to the bed.

Women have it hard as far as political equality, job rights, and equal pay. But as far as being free-thinkers, some of the freest thinkers we have are women. We already control the economy. The cosmetic industry alone, we could wreak havoc all over the place. Yeah. Can you imagine all the money Avon makes? And most of the people that use Avon faithfully—and I don't even like their products—are poor people. You hardly ever go into a poor home without seeing some kind of Avon product. They can't afford more expensive cosmetics. But I don't care how poor they are, they got Avon.

I don't feel any need to be liberated as a free-thinking individual. Contrary to popular opinion most hillbillies think for themselves. If women were satisfied with themselves as women, as people, as human beings, they then wouldn't confuse women's rights with people's rights. Women's lib is a middle-class movement and they better quit passing the buck.

I *need* a man. But not to depend on. I want a friend I can share everything with. I'd like to have a man to come home to me and sit down and eat beans and potatoes with me every night. We wouldn't have to starve, I can still work too.

I want a man that's as big as I am. A man I can't walk over. Someone who is willing to share the good and the bad. When I find him, I don't care if he digs outhouse holes for a living, I'm going to live with him.

You Don't Need to Be in That Mill

RUBY GREEN
HENDERSONVILLE, NORTH CAROLINA

I'm setting on the stoop of my company house
With my french harp in my mouth.
Doggone the day that I was born
To work in a mill down South.

The town of Hendersonville, North Carolina, is a study in generations. And class. Every summer at the first sign of a laurel bud blooming, the tourists flock to Hendersonville and the surrounding mountainsides. They come, young and old, in blue jeans and bermuda shorts, to bask in the fine mountain atmosphere and gape at Jump Off Rock.

The wealthier tourists fly in and make a beeline for their mountain A-frame chalets shaded beneath the tall pine and birch trees, secluded near lakes and mountain streams stocked with fish. The younger, less affluent tourists camp out in

Pisgah National Forest, washing their hip clothes in clear mountain streams.

Ruby Green waits tables in Hendersonville. She has been a waitress off and on for many years, ever since she left her job at the cotton mill. Most of the year-round residents of Hendersonville work in the cotton mills and factories for companies that discovered the town and its people long before the tourists.

Being exposed to tourists the way she is, waiting on their tables, cleaning up after them, and having traveled a little herself, Ruby understands all kinds of people, young and old, rich and poor. And she knows where she stands.

Ruby Green was born and raised around the cotton mills of Hendersonville. She spent twenty years in the weave room of a mill. All she has to show for those years in the mill is brown lung, a serious respiratory disease medically termed byssinosis. Like the coal miners' black lung, brown lung is caused by unclean working conditions. Cotton mill workers' lungs are gradually filled with the fine dust that comes off the cotton as it is carded and spun and wound into cotton fabric which is used to make clothing for all classes of people. The finished product is advertised as "Clean, Comfortable, Carefree Cotton" by the textile corporations who are polluting the lungs of mill workers daily.

There are not many statistics on brown lung in this country. However, it is known that thousands of mill workers have died from the disease, which shows its early symptoms as a bad cough and congestion in the bronchial tubes. Like black lung, it is a disease of slow suffocation.

No federal or state legislation has been passed to provide compensation to victims of brown lung and the textile corporations have done very little to prevent it. Although a handful of brown lung claims have been compensated, law does not provide compensation for its victims. And though there are ways of preventing brown lung, by steaming and washing the cotton before it goes through the carding process, these measures have not been taken by the textile corporations. There are other methods of keeping the air in cotton mills free of dust particles, but they all cost money. The corporations have finally admitted the existence of brown lung, but they are reluctant to spend the money to eradicate the disease in their cotton mills. Until they voluntarily eliminate the causes of it, or until they are forced to through federal legislation, thousands more mill workers will suffer and die.

Ruby Green uses the tips she makes as a waitress to help pay for the cost of her hospitalization whenever she has a bad coughing spell or difficulty in breathing. For Ruby, it is not only a matter of making a living; it is a matter of staying alive.

I stayed nine months out West. Stayed right out of Kent, Washington, out on the Pacific Highway.

I had gone from job to job, working at the cotton mill, and all that, having Donna Lee and Vince and working in the mill to raise them. I'd just had it up to here. So I just made up my mind that I was going to get away from that mill village. I said I wanted to go as far as I could get without getting out of the United States.

Well, this taxi driver I'd been dating, and this other taxi driver and his girl friend, they said to me about one o'clock on a Friday afternoon, they said, "Let's go to the State of Washington." And I said, "By God, *I'm* game!"

They said, "You're chicken-shit. You won't go." I said, "Hell, I *will* go." I went home and I said, "Mama, I'm leaving. Will you keep the kids till I get a job and a place to live? Then I'll send for them or come back and get them." Mama said yes. I packed my little suitcase and at four o'clock they picked me up and we were on our way.

We traveled for six days and nights. We got into Kent the next Friday. And nobody had a job, nobody knew nobody. I said, "I'm getting *me* a job." And I went out and found me one.

This was in '48, just in the beginning of October. I went to work as a waitress. This guy I went with, he finally got a job in the pickle factory. The other two, they never did get jobs.

One day the other guy took off, left, stole what money we had, took the car, and left the gal there with us. I was working and supporting them all for a while. My man didn't last long at the pickle factory.

Just as soon as I had made enough tips to give that gal money to get the bus, I got rid of her. Sent her back home. See, one day I caught her with my man.

He stayed there until right after New Year's, then I shipped him off too, cause he tried to choke me to death on New Year's Eve. But I beat him off with the poker. I got his clothes and set them out on the porch. Then I made him set down on the couch and I set there, held the poker over him all night. On New Year's Day, I went to work with my throat all marks on it. A couple weeks later, I'd made enough money, I give *him* the bus fare and sent *him* back to Hendersonville.

They were going to build a new big restaurant out

there on the Pacific Highway near Kent and they wanted me to live there and run it. That's when I came home. With the intention of getting my kids, taking them back there and running that restaurant.

When I got back home to Hendersonville, my sisters all pitched a fit that I owed it to my mama and daddy not to take the kids away. Said Mama and Daddy would die if I did that. So I decided to stay here then. And I went back to work in the cotton mill.

I was eighteen when I first went to work in the cotton mill. Back when my daddy and my sister Myrtle went to work, they were hiring kids fourteen years old.

Daddy went to work in the weave room and Myrtle worked in the spinning room. They went to work just at the tail end of the Depression. They'd go to work at six o'clock at night and got off at six in the morning. My daddy, he brought home twelve dollars and fifty cents a week.

We lived in that cotton mill village twenty-one years. They had company houses, and all you had in the houses was this little bitty wire that hangs down from the living room ceiling, with a bulb in it, and a fireplace in two of the rooms. And we had an old wood stove we brought with us.

Vince and Donna Lee were five and eight years old before the company ever put any decent toilets in the houses. We had plumbing; we had one cold-water spigot in the kitchen and one of them old toilets that the water run all the time in it. When you set on it and then got up it usually gave you a cold shower. Self-flusher, I reckon that's what they call it.

The houses, you could see the moon and the stars through the cracks. They weren't underpinned, just up on stilts. When we first moved there, when I was just a little bitty girl, I'd be so cold at night I'd just freeze, draw up in a knot. Mama would put me in the bed with her, try to get me warm.

The Company was owned by Captain Adger Smythe who came up here from Pelzer, South Carolina, to open this mill village. He owned Pelzer Mills and some others. He named the village here Balfour, after some place in England, something to do with his ancestors.

When Captain Smythe came here and built the mill village, he imported a whole bunch of them blackbirds from England and turned them loose over here. And they multiplied. Lord, I've seen them over there in the pastures, those pastures just black with them. I reckon that's as near as he could come to getting a raven, so he just got hisself an old blackbird.

He had this chauffeur, and for years, after the first frost, this chauffeur would drive old Captain Smythe all around the back behind the mill houses and he'd lay out a big bunch of collards on everybody's back porch.

He was a fine old man, Captain Smythe, and him and his heirs was just as nice as they could be to everybody. Course, they didn't hobnob with us none socially. He was out to make money in his business, and he didn't give you no gravy train. You worked, you sweated it out.

I remember when we first went to work at Balfour, I seen the time when Mama had nothing more to cook for supper except potatoes, and make gravy and a big pone of bread. But you didn't starve even on that. We ate much better than the majority of people around us.

There was a bunch of us that would run around together, drink and have a good time. One of the guys I went with was a Moody. That poor guy's dead now. He just lived too fast . . . fast women like me just got the best of him.

You wouldn't believe at the trips I made with this Moody guy, up and down the Greenville Mountain hauling liquor. That's all the Moodys ever did for a living was bootlegging. Why, my God, I've hid many a case of liquor and then scratched it out of the leaves.

Now, this brother of his, Fred Moody, he worked over here on the railroad and he fell off the train one day and the train, it cut his leg off. So Fred had a wooden leg. When we'd start out to go and drink, everybody hid their money in that hole in Fred's wooden leg. So if we got drunk, we wouldn't lose our money. Cause we knew Fred wasn't going to lose his leg. You'd've died seeing us sticking our fingers in there, in that hole in Fred's wooden leg, to get our money out.

Over there at the cotton mill, I worked in the weave shop, filling batteries. That's where you put the thread on the bobbin in the thing that turns it down to where it goes in the shuttle and then goes in the loom. The thread is on what they call a wooden quill and you filled those things up and put them in there. And then it turns and drops it in the shuttle where it goes back and forth in the loom.

People used snuff and chewed tobacco and they'd spit in the cans where my bobbins would drop. And if you come to a battery that something was wrong with, was knocking them out instead of putting them in the shuttle, it dropped down in the quill can. Then you had to reach down in there and pick those things up and put them back in there. Nine times out of ten, when you reached down in that can you got a handful of snuff or tobacco along with the filling.

The loom fixer, the machinist on the job, he went with his cheek just as full of tobacco as he could poke it. And every other can he come to he spit in that quill can. I have stood there and cussed that man till I'd be blue in the face. He'd just stand over there and laugh at me. They had wooden floors then and most of them would just spit in the floor. So if you didn't get it in your hands, you stepped in it.

They had a lot of dust in there. All this lint and stuff, it just foamed. And they took these blow pipes and would blow the stuff off the looms to keep it out of the cloth, cause if some of that stuff got in there it made these lumps, hard places in the cloth. A lot of the lint and dust went into our lungs. There was a lot of it you'd breathe.

Then Kimberly-Clark bought the mill, and after a while they started into weaving gauze for Kotex, feminine napkins. All we made was the raw gauze for the Kotex and it was sent other places to sterilize and bleach.

All this time I worked in the mills, they always used these blow pipes to blow this lint and stuff off the looms. Well, maybe I'd be standing in this alley of looms filling this battery or weaving, and this guy comes down the alley with this air hose blowing it off. Well, he just fills your face full. I've picked it out of my eyes, hair, face, dug it out of my ears.

Even the humidity in the mill would make it worse. I knew it was making my cough worse, and my doctor kept preaching to me that it was. Every time he saw me he fussed at me. He'd say, "You don't need to be in that mill." He started on me the first time I went to see him when I'd only been in the mill four or five years. Started right then telling me to get out. Course, these doctors can tell you to do all these things for your health, but they don't tell you where to get the money to do it with. They set back there and take your money for telling you that. Yet, I was having to make a living and support my family. My doctor says to me that all that stuff I breathed in the mill wasn't doing my lungs any good, that being in that stuff, working in it, was irritating and agitating it. But he never would say that working in the mill caused it. I never was in any other kind of irritant but the dust in the mill.

I've been having these coughs and breathing problems several times a year. All the time I worked in the mill, I was in the hospital three or four times a year for my breathing and all this congestion in my bronchial tubes. The doctor still gives me medication and injections for it. I was just down to him two weeks ago and had some for this spree. He's used this Bird machine on me ever since they got it over there at the hospital. It's this thing that's got medication and oxygen combined. You hold the tube in your mouth and suck it into your lungs. They use it on people that have this breathing problem. If I thought then that the years I worked over there caused me to get brown lung, I would have been the first to be jumping on everybody about it. But it just never occurred to me then.

A lot of women in the mill took pills to keep them going, but I didn't. I don't know just exactly what they were taking. Most of what I saw people take was Stanbacks and B.C.'s. They just ate those things. People was taking them just every time you turned around, just coming and going. Goody Powders, my God, they took them by the cases. Take one of them darn things and drink a Coke with it. I've seen them take them by the barrels.

I was getting paid a dollar and twenty-five an hour after I'd worked there awhile. Now, talking union—you go over there now and say union and you'll get shot. Kimberly-Clark has got unions in some places, but we don't talk union here.

After I quit the mill, I worked eight years' waitress work. There's not that much money in waitress work here. Most of the tourists that come here come with a two-dollar bill and a shirt and they don't change either one till they leave. The City Fathers advertise this area as tourist potential and then the local businesses jack up their prices on the poor home folks. The local working class of people don't like it. Yet, we're stupid enough to elect the officials that do this to us. Well, as long as we vote these people in, we just have to back our ears and accept it. And this applies to any community. Until the people get up on their high horses and get sense enough to vote the right way, and all these different things we could do to change the way it is . . . Just like me. I sit right here and bitch up a storm. But, do I get out and do anything about it? No. Neither does anybody else.

Now, these antipoverty workers, the hell of it is, they come in here supposed to be doing all this good . . . now,

I'm not knocking them, cause there's a great potential if they'd do what they're supposed to do . . . but they come into these poverty-stricken areas looking down their damn noses like they smell shit. Now, a Rebel, a good old mountain person, has got too damn much pride to swaller that. I don't care how hard up he is.

Now my husband, Adger, the Greens are part English and part Indian. Look at his nose, look at his cheekbones, and then just watch his attitude. If he ain't got Indian, I'll eat him. Why, when we go up to town, he walks in front of me and I walk a few steps behind. Stoic, that's what he is.

We're the backbone, just like the women of the West. We're the backbone of *this* part of the country.

Have You Ever Been
on a Mountaintop?

NANCY KINCAID
FAYETTEVILLE, WEST VIRGINIA

Down in West Virginia you can see them roll
Down that narrow valley loaded down with coal.
It's the Strip Mine Special, a hundred coal cars long,
And that train keeps moving, but the people are gone.

Nancy Kincaid has a message for the coal companies. She has
been trying to get the message across for several years, but so
far they have not heeded her words. And if they had, perhaps
the disaster at Buffalo Creek could have been prevented.

Nancy lives near Buffalo Creek, West Virginia, where on
February 26, 1972, a dam owned by the Pittston Coal Company burst and carried its murderous waters through Logan
County, killing some one hundred twenty-five men, women,
and children and injuring thousands more. The dam was made
of the slag which comes out of the coal mines, waste which

can be seen piled high all around the coal camps of Southern Appalachia. The people who were killed were coal miners, both active and disabled, their wives and their children. Their names have been added to the list of thousands of hillbillies trapped and killed by the criminally negligent coal companies in Southern Appalachia.

Nancy lives in Fayetteville, West Virginia, a community ravaged by strip mining. Her house is new, built by herself and her husband, Harvey. They live there with their seven children. They do not know how long they will be able to stay in their new house before the strippers force them out as they did once before.

Strip mining started in Southern Appalachia when the coal companies discovered it was cheaper and easier to tear away the shallower seams of coal directly from the mountainside. And as they tear and as they bulldoze the mountains the land is ravaged, the animals are left to die from exposure and starvation, people's homes are destroyed, and the land is left to "reclaim" itself.

Stripping is an easy way to make quick money if you don't have a conscience. And the strippers are working twenty-four hours a day in West Virginia, Virginia, Tennessee, and Kentucky because they know that the pressure by people like Nancy Kincaid to stop their destruction is constantly building. And as they doze and dynamite the mountains down, each attempt to prohibit their destruction is coldly rejected by the federal government.

Strip mining has been good to some politicians. West Virginia State Senator Tracy Hilton owns his own strip mine and is so proud of it that he flies foreign reporters in by helicopter to view his land. He does not tell them, however, that the land they see is not in fact the stripped land but actually a showcase plot of land he has developed to fool visitors. But Senator Hilton is not fooling the people of Fayette County.

Nancy has been trying to stop the strip mining, despite the attempts of politicians to convince her and her neighbors that stripping is "good" for the land and the animals.

In 1971, flanked by Senator Ken Hechler and some of her neighbors, Nancy spoke in Washington, D.C., to the Congress Against Strip Mining. But the stripping has not stopped and as the danger grows Nancy keeps fighting to end the destruction of her land. If people will only listen to her they will learn why spoil banks, slag heaps, and dams are deadly. If they listen hard enough they will hear about our land and what is happening to it and what must be done to save it from destruction.

Gentlemen:

I don't believe there could be anyone that would like to see the strip mines stopped any more than my husband and myself. It just seems impossible that something like this could happen to us twice in the past three and one half years of time. We have been married for thirteen years and worked real hard at having a nice home that was ours and paid for, with a nice size lot of one acre. Over the thirteen years, we remodeled this house a little at a time and paid for it as we worked and did the work mostly ourselves. The house was located about a quarter of a mile off the road up Glenco Hollow at Kincaid, Fayette County, West Virginia, where it used to be a nice, clean neighborhood.

Then the strippers came four years ago with their big

machinery and TNT. I know that these men need jobs and need to make a living like everyone else, but I believe there could be a better way of getting the coal out of these mountains. Have you ever been on a mountaintop and looked down and seen about five different strips on one mountain in one hollow?

My husband owns a Scout Jeep and he can get to the top of the strip mines with the Scout. I would like to invite you to come and visit us sometime and go for a ride with us. It would make you sick to see the way the mountains are destroyed.

First they send in the loggers to strip all the good timber out and then they come with their bulldozers. If their engineers make a mistake in locating the coal they just keep cutting away until they locate the seam of coal. When the rains come and there isn't anything to stop the drainage, the mountains slide, and the spoil banks fall down to the next spoil bank and so on until the whole mountain slides. There is a small creek in the hollow and when the spring rains come, its banks won't hold the water.

So where does it go?—into people's yards, into their wells, under and into their houses. You have rocks, coal, and a little bit of everything in your yards. When the strippers came they started behind our house in the fall sometime before November. There was a hollow behind our house and we asked them not to bank the spoil the way they did, because we knew what would happen when the spring rains came. My father-in-law lived beside us and the property all ran together in a nice green lawn—four acres.

But the rains came in the spring and the spoil bank broke and the water and debris came into our property every time it rained. It would only take a few minutes of rain and this is what we had for three years.

Then the damage comes to your house because of so much dampness. The doors won't close, the foundation sinks and cracks the walls in the house, your tile comes up off your floors, your walls mold, even your clothes in your closets. Then your children stay sick with bronchial trouble, then our daughter takes pneumonia—X-rays are taken, primary T.B. shows up on the X-ray. This is in July of two years ago. About for a year this child laid sick at home. In the meantime we have already filed suit with a lawyer in Oak Hill when the water started coming in on us, but nothing happens. For three years we fight them for our property—$10,000. The lawyer settles out of court for $4,500. By the time his fee comes out and everything else we have to pay, we have under $3,000 to start over with.

So what do we have to do? Doctor's orders, move out for child's sake and health. We sell for a little of nothing —not for cash, but for rent payments, take the $3,000 and buy a lot on the main highway four miles up the road toward Oak Hill.

The $3,000 goes for the lot, digging of a well and a down payment on a new house. Here we are in debt for thirty years on a new home built and complete by the first of September. We moved the first part of September and was in this house *one month* and what happens? The same strip company comes up the road and puts a blast off and damages the new house—$1,400 worth. When they put one blast off that will crack the walls in your house, the foundation cracked the carport floor straight across in two places, pull a cement stoop away from the house and pull the grout out of the ceramic tile in the bathroom. This is what they can get by with.

How do they live in their $100,000 homes and have a clear mind, I'll never know. To think of the poor people who have worked hard all their lives and can't start over like we did. They have to stay in these hollows and be scared to death every time it rains. I know by experience the many nights I have stayed up and listened to the water pouring off the mountains and the rocks tumbling off the hills.

I remember one time when the strippers put a blast off up the hollow a couple years ago and broke into one of the old mines that had been sealed off for 30 years. They put their blast off and left for the evening. Around seven o'clock that evening it started. We happened to look up the hollow, and thick mud—as thick as pudding—was coming down the main road in the hollow and made itself to the creek and stopped the creek up until the creek couldn't even flow.

The water was turned up into the fields where my husband keeps horses and cattle. I called the boss and told him what was happening and the danger we were in and what did he say? "There isn't anything I can do tonight. I'll be down tomorrow." I called the agriculture and they told us, whatever we did, not to go to bed that night because of the water backed up in those mines for miles.

This is just some of the things that happen around a strip mine neighborhood. But they can get by with it, unless they are stopped. Even if they are stopped it will take years for the trees and grass—what little bit they put on them—to grow enough to keep the water back and stop the slides.

Mr. & Mrs. Harvey Kincaid

The above is a letter of testimony written by Nancy and Harvey Kincaid which was read before the West Virginia State Legislature by legislator Si Galperin to introduce the Anti-Strip-mining Bill which was later passed by the state. The letter was read by Nancy in Washington, D.C., when she represented West Virginia at the Congress Against Strip Mining.

When we moved to the hollow in '57, there was no stripping being done. But they had their first seam there. This hollow had a deep mine about thirty-five years ago. Then about five years ago they started the stripping.

We'd been fighting to get a road up the hollow, a black-top road. In the wintertime the kids would have to walk up the road to school with the mud up to their ankles. In the summertime they were always surrounded by dust. So we asked and asked for a road. But they wouldn't give us one. After a while, we gave up on it.

Then they started with the blacktop. We knew that the strippers were coming. Harv says to me, "You mark my word. Within a month they'll be here." And they were.

Used to, on Sundays, people would come up the road to picnic because it was so beautiful in the hollow. The properties would all run together in beautiful lawns. Just about everybody would have a horse and the kids would ride up and down the hollow on their horses. But now, nobody goes there anymore. Now the hollow has no hard road. When they finished stripping in it they put "red dog" on it. That's the old slag that burns in the slate dumps. They covered the road with that.

Mostly everybody in Glenco Hollow's related to each other. There was at least ten houses up in the hollow and double rows of houses right at the front of the hollow. When the strippers began stripping the mountains, the water would come down the hollow and block the main highway off. The water'd run halfway up the cars.

It used to be that the kids could keep fish, catfish, and minnows in the creeks. Now you can see the rocks in the creek where the acid has run off the mountains, off the limestone rocks. The rocks in the creek are reddish-looking, like they're rusted. There's nothing living in the creek now.

One of our Representatives from West Virginia was in Washington, D.C., speaking for strip mining when I was there to speak against it. He said that the only bad fault he knew about stripping was that it destroyed the land. I got to laughing about that. I mean, what *more?* He said, "They talk about the little animals, say it's destroying the little animals. But this is good for the animals, the strip mining, because it lets the sun shine in on them."

I thought I'd crack up when he said that. How stupid can anybody be? When they go so far down from the mountaintop and then cut a circle all the way around the mountain, those animals can't get down. So they're left up there to die unless there's some supply of water and food. If there's not, there's no possible way they can live.

Our house was surrounded by water. The mountain behind us got so bad where the two banks joined together to make a hollow, they just pushed the banks together to make a spoil. But the spoil bank broke and the rains rushed off that mountain in back of us and down into the creek in front of us. Eventually, all the spoil washed down upon us. We didn't know which way to run.

We had to keep digging to keep the water off us. Each time we'd dig a ditch, it would rain and fill back up with silt and gradually come back into flat land. So we just had to keep digging. Many a time Harvey missed work in the mines just because he was trying to keep the water off of us.

The strip company kept promising they would build us a dam, but they never did. They just piled the dirt all around our house. They built the dirt up so much all around the house that in the back of the house there was only about three or four inches of foundation above the ground.

There was one man, the water would run down his property. It had oil in it from the trucks used on the strip mine. And that water would run all around his well and into it and contaminated his drinking water.

I got to thinking, "Well." People would tell me not to do anything, not to say anything. But I was aggravated from the time they first started tearing up our road and refused to replace it.

We would ask the company to keep the water off us.

They would say it wasn't their fault, that it was an "act of God." My father-in-law said to them, "Is it an act of God that told you to go up there and tear the mountains up and let the water come down on us?"

There's an old couple that lives near the strip. This old man is in his eighties and he has to get out there and dig out culverts all the time to keep the water from hitting their house and washing them away.

There's people like this lady over here who had a rock to come clear through the roof of her house. My boy came home from school one day and said, "Mama, a rock fell on Mary Jane's house. You ought to go see about it." It was the first time anybody had said anything to me about getting involved.

Well, I went over to see the woman. When I first entered the house she said, "Oh, they fixed it, it's done with and repaired." I said, "Do you know they've done that to cover up? This is Mr. Tracy Hilton's work himself." I believe because this was a Colored family they thought they could get away with it.

She was in the kitchen when it happened. She has eight children and she was standing near the cook stove washing clothes. She never ironed anything on washday. Then she thought, "Mary Jane needs a pair of slacks to wear to school tomorrow." So she took the slacks across the room to the ironing table. Right then the rock came crashing through the ceiling right where she had been standing. This rock was bigger than a basketball. It came through the roof, knocked down the beams in the kitchen, and crashed down on top of her coal stove, just crashed into pieces.

Well, she said it was just like the other blasts. First you get the tremors like an earthquake and then you get the concussion of it. It's like it takes the walls out of your house, lifts them out and sets them back in. Then you feel the ground shaking and then you get the "BAM!" After that, you can look out the window and see orange smoke going up in the air and you know where they're blasting at.

This woman, she could see the rocks crashing down over the mountains, one mountain to the next. The stones come down so hard they actually imbedded themselves in the ground around the house. But this one hit the house, and so they classified *this* one as an accident.

There were so many ways we were in danger from the strip mine. Harvey works in the deep mines about twenty miles from here and some nights we'd have to be at home alone, me and the kids, when he was at work. When Sissy got sick, I didn't know what I would do. I knew she couldn't be wet. So Harvey took the car and parked it up above the house at a higher place. He told us to run to it whenever the water got so bad.

After the blast went off at this house, our second home, I thought, "Oh no! This can't be happening to us again." And, do you know, I stood there in our living room *laughing* because I just couldn't believe this could be happening again to us. And just living in our new home for one month and having this to happen.

I remember the day so plain: I was shaking the throw rugs and as I walked through the doorway the blast went off. And I knew what had happened before I even looked. The walls in each room were cracked, the blocks in the foundation of the house were cracked, the grout was out of the tile in the bathroom. But I would never have believed it would crack the carport and pull the front steps which were bolted to the house away from it. The ability to laugh only lasts so long.

So I called the Oak Hill newspaper. They said the best thing I could do was to sit down and write a letter to the legislators down in the Capitol in Charleston.

So it was real early one morning and all my kids was in school. I didn't have the five foster children yet. I was thinking about how we had took every dime of the three thousand dollars we had got to start over with and now this to happen to the second house. So I set down with notebook paper and a pencil. I must have poured my whole heart out because by the time I'd finished, I had eight notebook pages full.

I thought, "Why take the time to copy it over in ink? You'll never send it." So I stuck the pages in an envelope and put it in the mailbox as quick as I could. And all that day I kept thinking, "Harvey hasn't read it. Oh my gosh, he'll kill me, what have I said?" So I told Harvey when he got home what I had done.

The men who work with Harvey down at the mines began asking Harvey were we the ones that all the damage happened to. Said it was on the NBC news on the television. And said that I had introduced the Anti-Strip-mining Bill into the legislature with the letter I had wrote.

When Harvey come home he said, "*What* in this world have you put in that letter?" I said, "Well, I just told the truth." But there was lots of things that I'd left out.

I would stand at the window looking out. I'd see the

rocks coming down and I'd say, "Will you just tell me how they can do it?" And I'd be so heartbroken. Harvey'd say, "Well, *I* don't know how they can do it! I just know they can get by with it." I'd say, "I don't see how they can come in here and destroy people's property and get by with it. As hard as we've worked on it . . ." There were so many times like that.

There's a showplace at Cannelton, West Virginia, for the company to bring the politicians. They actually have a fence up there and when they are supposed to show a politician "reclaimed" land, they put cattle up there. But it's a fake.

There was this reporter from Germany, Peter Burke. Well, Tracy Hilton got ahold of him first, to show him *his* side of the mountain. Tracy's a senator and he owns a big strip company. Well, he was going to show this reporter the "reclaimed" strip down in the valley. So he took him in his helicopter, showed him the fake "strip," took him up to Pipestem for dinner and then flew him to Honey Rock, the hotel in Beckley.

Well then, the reporter came down here. All he could talk about was . . . "You know, it's called sort of . . . you know." You know how Germans talk. He says, "It was publicity, you know." I said, "Yeah, I know."

We took Peter Burke early that afternoon to show him the real strip. We got back down out of the mountains about nine o'clock when it was just getting dark. He stood down here in the driveway and said, "You know, I believe that Tracy Hilton was making a fool of me."

Well, he sat down here in the kitchen. And I thought, "Well, what in the world does he eat?"

I asked him if he'd like some cheese. He said, "Ya." So then I asked him if he'd like some lettuce. He said ya, he'd take the lettuce. Then I said, "Would you like some mayonnaise or salad dressing?" He said, "*Nooo*. In my nation it never been in*ven*ted." He put butter on his bread instead of mayonnaise.

"You know," he said, "your country . . . when we got here and stayed in Washington, D.C., one of our photographers was going down the street in a car and somebody shot at him. Actually *shot* at him! He went up to a police officer and the officer said, 'Oh, this happens over here all the time.' "

Peter told us they had strip mines in Germany but that over there they reclaimed the land right. He said, "I've seen it. It can be done right." But it cost so much to reclaim the land that very little stripping is done in Germany.

When we were standing up there on the mountain with Peter, he said, "You know, your country is getting ready for a revolution . . ."

Without Anger
There Won't Be Any Change

Each time I read over the stories of these women, I am filled with a sense of failure. I feel that somehow I failed to capture their intensity and strength and the emotion with which they recall the cruel experiences of their lives. No words can do justice to the feelings of these women born to struggle. Even as they risk disaster every day of their lives they are filled with a sense of hope that seems extraordinary in the light of the history of mountain people.

Nor are there words to describe my feelings about the conditions that have caused people to live such desperate lives. I hope the stories of these nineteen women will make other people angry too. Anger is what is needed, anger at the conditions of an oppressive society and at the people who keep it that way. Without anger there won't be any change.

I'll never forget the day Myra Watson got indoor plumbing in her house and the pride she felt because she had finally saved up enough money to have it installed. Why did she have to wait sixty-four years for indoor plumbing? Why did Granny Hager have to walk mile after mile in the rain and snow from her house to the Social Security office before she was granted the benefits she was due? Why do the women in Goose Creek, Kentucky, have to pick over clothes rejected by the Salvation Army when they and their families need something to wear? And why is it that Shirley Dalton, her husband and seven children are forced to live on thirty-two dollars a week when they can't find work and have to draw welfare? Who is responsible for Artie Chandler's nervous breakdown? Why does Jack Smith have to spend the rest of his life in a wheelchair?

I remember a six-week-old baby girl who died of malnutrition because local doctors refused to treat her. The mother was too poor to pay a doctor and too weak from malnutrition herself to nurse the baby. When the baby died, they had to bury her in a wooden box out in the back yard of their tenant farmer's shack. They couldn't afford a funeral.

I remember a family of nine who lived for a week on a loaf of bread and a jar of mayonnaise. And a working-class family whose house was burned to the ground by company-hired nightriders because the woman and her husband were organizing a union in a local factory.

I remember the faces of the Hyden widows shortly after their men had been murdered in the Hurricane Creek Massacre, faces filled with pain, anger in their eyes. And the smug composure of the coal operators and county officials who pretended to be sorry.

After living in the Southern mountains for almost ten years, I have come to believe that hillbilly people are some of the most maligned people in America. And although I have never lived in the abject poverty most hillbillies have to endure, I am not free to ignore these conditions, any more than a person who reads about these women can ignore the existence of colonialism in Southern Appalachia.

Everybody has an obligation to defend his or her right to dignity and self-respect, to a decent job, good health, food, clothing, and shelter. The cooperative efforts of oppressed people and other people who want change will make the task of defending human rights easier. The conditions that allow people to live in desperation affect each one of us, morally and physically, and threaten the well-being of future generations. These conditions must not only be exposed; they must be changed.

Some of the more sophisticated tactics used against people who struggle are seen in the recent history of the Southern mountains. People who fight for safe living conditions are murdered en masse like the people in Buffalo Creek, West Virginia. Miners who fight for safe working conditions are punished by death in the mines, or, like Jock Yablonski, his wife and daughter, are murdered while they sleep. These are not accidents; they are the direct result of the greed of the wealthy and powerful people who control American society.

What can people do to create a more just society? I think they can start by examining their own lives and discovering how they are being used to sustain corruption and oppression. Then they can begin the long hard work of resisting.

Poor people must learn to resist the unfair and illegal tactics used against them by the federal and state programs which are supposed to be helping them out of poverty. Working-class people must resist unfair treatment on the job, unsafe working conditions, low wages, and discrimination in seniority rights.

The burden of changing a corrupt society falls most heavily upon those who are most oppressed, people like these hillbilly women. When you live at the very bottom, the pressure from the folks on top never lets up. It is obvious from the stories of these women that poor and working people are resisting that pressure. But the cooperative effort needs to be even stronger.

There are several organizations in the Southern mountains that are working for change. Poor and working-class mountain people can get involved in the efforts of these grassroots organizations. People outside the mountains can get involved too. They can give some of their time, their skills and support to these organizations.

At the end of this book I have listed the names and addresses of several grassroots organizations in Southern Appalachia along with a brief summary of what these organizations are doing. If the stories of these women have made you angry, your anger can be converted into action by contacting some of these groups and finding out what you can do to assist them.

I have also included a list of newspapers and periodicals published in Southern Appalachia, their addresses and subscription rates. If you want to know more about the struggles of hillbilly people, you might subscribe to some of them.

There are some other things people outside the mountains can do to assist hillbilly people in their struggle for human dignity. They can refuse to give their time and skills to the large corporations that are underpaying and overworking mountain people, the same corporations that are slowly murdering coal miners and mill workers while they extract millions of dollars from the labor of mountain people and ravage their land.

If you have money, you can buy stock, individually or together with friends, in these corporations and then turn that stock over to a grassroots organization in the mountains. Or make direct financial contributions to grassroots and migrant organizations.

Exposing the struggles of these nineteen hillbilly women is only a small part of a larger effort by many people to change the living and working conditions of hillbilly people. Hopefully these stories will serve their purpose. I did not write this book to be read and then set up on the shelf to gather dust. I wrote it with the hope that it will generate some action from the people who read it. Read it, put it up on the shelf and then begin, like these proud women, to resist.

APPENDIX

Grassroots Organizations and Publications in Southern Appalachia

Following is a list of some grassroots organizations and publications in the Southern mountains, a brief summary of what the organizations are doing and what you might do to help them, and addresses and subscription rates to magazines and newspapers which deal with the problems of people in Southern Appalachia.

ORGANIZATIONS

Council of the Southern Mountains
Drawer N
Clintwood, Virginia 24228

The Council of the Southern Mountains is the only region-wide grassroots organization in Appalachia. It links people in local communities and counties across the mountains in strategic ways in order to help make the work of local groups stronger. The Council is actually a "council of local organizations" made up of representatives of community groups from all the mountain states. Representatives from these community groups meet together several weekends a year to discuss each other's work and to combine organizations into coalitions. Together, these community groups work on such issues as the special problems of Black Appalachians, needed welfare reforms, failures of local health services, black lung compensation, miners', textile and industrial workers' health and safety, inadequate educational services, strip mining, labor disputes, jobs and economic development, migrants who have been forced to leave the mountains in search of jobs, and Appalachian studies. The Council also prints literature and announcements and publishes a monthly magazine called *Mountain Life & Work* (see publications list). The counsel needs financial support to allow this coalition of grassroots organizations to work and grow together. Donations are tax exempt.

Highlander Research and Education Center
Route 1, Box 245A
New Market, Tennessee 37820

The Highlander Center plans and conducts adult education workshops on leadership training, and problem-solving on the community level for poor and working Southerners. The work of the Center is rooted in the Highlander Folk School, which began in the 1930s as a labor school, to teach workers how to organize and run their unions. By the 1940s, Highlander was becoming more involved with the problems of farmers, and during the fifties and sixties with the civil rights movement. Highlander's Appalachian self-education program is becoming more central to their overall program. A main objective is to identify groups throughout Appalachian communities with common problems and to set up residential workshops at the Center to permit representatives from several groups to work together on solutions. Highlander concentrates primarily on workshops and small group discussions, with outside resource people who usually donate their services. Each workshop is set up in response to a request from community organizations. At the present time from six hundred to seven hundred persons are enrolled each year in Highlander workshops or training sessions. Highlander also sponsors music workshops which concentrate on the songs of poor and working-class people and their struggles. Eighty per cent of Highlander's support comes from private donations. These donations are tax exempt. Highlander could also use books and literature on contemporary social problems.

Mud Creek Health Project
Box 34
Beaver, Kentucky 41604

The Mud Creek Health Project represents four years of work by residents of Floyd County, Kentucky. It was begun to provide an alternative to the poor health care in Floyd County. The project is a clinic which is staffed by two part-time doctors and a secretary, and is run by a community-controlled Board.

The purposes of the clinic are: (1) to help poor people gain decent health care; (2) to work for the improvement of the health and welfare of poor people in the region; (3) to assist members in need in all ways possible to obtain good quality health care; (4) to educate all people about the need for better health care for poor people in rural areas; (5) to establish and maintain a medical facility which will serve poor people in the area. They need money to hire nurses, a bookkeeper and other staff, to maintain supplies and pay for equipment. Donations are tax exempt.

Model Valley Industrial Development Corporation
Clairfield, Tennessee 37715

The Model Valley Industrial Development Corporation is a not-for-profit group organized to facilitate healthy growth in the rural communities of Clairborne and Campbell counties in Tennessee and in Bell and Whitley counties in Kentucky.

Basically Model Valley programs have three aspects: (1) a basic industrial development plan inducing a labor survey and job retraining program to create jobs and keep the labor force "home"; (2) a folk arts program to find an organized way for people to increase, share, and market their craft skills; and, (3) health programs in five communities that have organized primary health clinics to serve many sick people with comprehensive, permanent health staffing and facilities.

Without at least a minimum of funds and basic personnel Model Valley would not function. It has been operating now for five years. To keep it going Model Valley needs financial contributions and skilled personnel.

Appalachian Film Workshop
Write to: APPAL-SHOP
Box 743
Whitesburg, Kentucky 41858

The Appal-shop is a group of young Appalachians portray-
ing their history, culture, and heritage through the media of
film, videotape, still photography, and audio recording. For the
first time, Appalachian people have the opportunity to show
their world as they see it, expressing the positive aspects as well
as the negative areas. As they capture the uniqueness of the
mountain experience, a strong Appalachian consciousness
emerges.

Operating funds come from film, video, and photographic
contract work; from sales and rentals of their eight original
films, and some grants from private foundations and churches.
Their productions are for rent or purchase. Purchases can be
made through their catalogue which they will send you if you
write them and request one.

Black Appalachian Commission
52 Fairlie St.
Room 305
Atlanta, Georgia 30303

The precentage of Black people living in the Southern Appalachian Mountains is very small compared to other areas of
the South (in the area of Appalachia covered in this book,
Black Appalachians number about 6.5 per cent). Black Appalachians have their own unique problems, being such a small
minority in an area mostly populated by White Anglo Saxons.
These problems include racial discrimination, isolation from
the Black cultural heritage and complicating that, the problems
of dealing with the unique culture of Black people in the
mountains.

The Black Appalachian Commission is attempting to break
down isolation and increase communication among Black communities in the mountains. It should be emphasized that Black
Appalachians are not only struggling with the usual problems

of racial discrimination but are also struggling under the same conditions as White hillbillies in the factories, mines and mills in the Southern mountains. A study conducted by the National Urban League in 1972 shows that Black Appalachians are even more poverty stricken than most White people in the mountains.

The Black Appalachian Commission is also attempting to look at the attitudes and culture of Black people in the mountains. The Commission could use financial support. They are especially in need of financial assistance to sponsor a conference on Black Appalachians. They need printing equipment to publish a newsletter which they will distribute among Black communities in the mountains. They could use research assistants in the area of Black cultural heritage and especially the cultural heritage of Black Appalachians. Tax exempt.

Appalachian South Folklife Center
Pipestem, West Virginia 25979

The Appalachian South Folklife Center, commonly known as "Pipestem," was begun as a folklife center which would have a reservoir of folk culture and folk history of Appalachia. It is now developing an extensive library and museum of regional history. The Center is also used for an annual folk festival, various meetings, and a children's summer camp. The staff of the Center is trying to awaken an understanding and appreciation for mountain culture and the social and economic problems of Appalachia. The educational work of the Center is designed to try to stimulate young people to be concerned with staying in the mountains and doing something about mountain people's problems. Tax exempt.

McCaysville Industries
McCaysville, Georgia 30555

This is the women's sewing factory that developed after the 1966 wildcat strike against Levi-Strauss in Blue Ridge, Georgia. The women own, operate, and manage the factory themselves.

They need help in marketing their products (presently women's dresses), in designing new garments for sale, and money to purchase more sewing machines so they can employ more women.

Appalachian Identity Center
1324 Walnut Street
Cincinnati, Ohio 45215

The Appalachian Identity Center has two basic purposes. First, they are concerned with the immediate problem of providing hillbilly migrant youth living in the Over the Rhine slum with a safe place to get together. The folks who run the Center are dedicated to preventing gang fights in the streets by giving young people an alternative place to go other than the streets. Second, the Center is trying to educate hillbilly migrant youth about their culture and heritage. They need educational material, especially material concerning the Southern mountains, they need recreational equipment, and they need money to sponsor trips to the mountains where hillbilly migrant youths can find their roots. They could also use financial contributions to repair their building and help pay their staff.

Brotherhood of Southern Indians
c/o Hawk Littlejohn
Louisville, Tennessee 37777

This recently organized group of Indians describes themselves and their organization beautifully in their own words: "A single twig breaks but the bundle of twigs is strong." They go on to say, "We the Brotherhood of Southern Indians unite to reclaim our heritage. We unite to regain our birthright, our civil rights, our right to live in dignity and rest in our mother earth in peace."

The Brotherhood of Southern Indians invites anyone who is

one quarter Indian or more to unite with them if they are in agreement with the stated purposes of the Brotherhood.

The Brotherhood is in need of financial assistance. Presently they are supporting their organization mostly by personal contributions and through contributions made by its members. They are looking for an offset press. They are also interested in receiving historical documents, copies of treaties and other authentic material relating to Indians, their culture and their struggle. Donations are tax exempt.

PUBLICATIONS

Mountain Life & Work
Drawer N
Clintwood, Virginia 24228

This monthly magazine published by the Council of the Southern Mountains features regional news, analysis, and reports by community groups and labor groups in Appalachia. The Council also operates a bookstore which has an extensive stock of books and records on Appalachia. Their price list is available upon request and is an excellent guide to available materials. The subscription rate to *Mountain Life & Work* is $10 a year, which includes membership in the Council. The address of the Council's bookstore is CSM Bookstore, C.P.O. 2307, Berea, Kentucky 40403.

People's Appalachia
Route 8, Box 292K
Morgantown, West Virginia 26505

People's Appalachia is a magazine which deals with most of the critical issues confronting Appalachian people. Subjects covered range from in-depth analyses of the energy elite to

Appalachian studies, migration, people's history, and guides to resources. Subscriptions are free, but contributions are needed to support their work.

Foxfire
Rabun Gap, Georgia 30568

Foxfire is a quarterly magazine concerned mainly with mountain traditions and culture and the preservation of Appalachian skills and experiences. The magazine is produced by a staff of high school students at the Rabun Gap school. Recent issues have included such articles as "Witches, Boogers and Haints," "Dressing and Cooking Game," "Ginseng," "Mountain Recipes," and "The End of Moonshining as a Fine Art." Subscriptions are $5 a year.

Mountain Eagle
120 West Main Street
Whitesburg, Kentucky 41858

This is probably the nearest thing Appalachia has to a regional weekly newspaper. While it provides local coverage for Whitesburg and Letcher County, it also carries extensive news and analysis of regional interest. Subscriptions are $5 a year outside Letcher County, Kentucky.

Appalachian Movement Press
1600 8th Avenue
Huntington, West Virginia 25705

"AMP" publishes a series of pamphlets on the mountains. Since it began in 1970 it has published dozens of articles in pamphlet form concerning the present-day social and economic and political status of the Appalachian region and also pamphlets on the history of the mountains. Subscribers receive all publications. A catalogue is available on request. Subscription rates are $25 for wealthy Appalachians, $7.50 for working Appalachians, $5 for students in Appalachia, and free for unemployed Appalachians. If you live outside the mountains, write them for information on a subscription rate.

Cut Cane Associates
P. O. Box 98
Mineral Bluff, Georgia

Cut Cane Associates publishes about six pamphlets a year. Some of their material includes a guide to mountain music and where to find it, a suggested course catalogue for an Appalachian People's University, pamphlets on strategies for community organizations, facts about brown lung, and stories about life and conditions in mill and mining towns. Publications are free to poor Appalachians and community groups. Write to them for their catalogue which lists prices of pamphlets.

Kattelagatee
c/o Committee of Southern Churchmen
P. O. Box 12044
Nashville, Tennessee 37212

This quarterly publication deals with special issues concerning Southern Appalachia, its land and its people. Currently, the subscription rate is $2–$4 per year for four issues.

Black Lung Bulletin and *United Mine Workers Journal*
1437 K Street, N.W.
Washington, D.C. 20005

Now that Arnold Miller has been elected to the presidency of the UMW, it looks as if the Black Lung Association, which publishes the *Black Lung Bulletin*, will be working directly with the UMW. The two publications will probably merge to form a comprehensive analysis of what is happening in the Southern coal fields as well as in other mines around America. Write to the UMW for information about their publications and subscription rates for folks who don't work in the mines. Presently the subscription rate is $1 a year for nonmembers of the UMWA.

Coal Patrol
National Press Building, Room 737
1437 K Street, N.W.
Washington, D.C. 20004

This independent news-weekly provides news and commentary on coal related developments from the point of view of the abuse of the land and people by labor, industry and government. The subscription rates are $7.50 a year for individuals and $15 for organizations.